Did I Miss Anything?

Acknowledgements

To my wife Anita, who translated my handwritten scrawl into readable print and offered some helpful hints along the lengthy way.

To all past and present Tale Spinners, my writing group, thanks for your encouragement and critiques, with a special nod to our leader, Irene Miller.

My thanks to the Minnetonka Senior Center for providing us wth a meeting room.

1
Watch Out For Those French Girls

I WAS STANDING on the afterwell deck of the *S.S. West Chatala*. As I looked eastward, through the misty light of dawn, I could make out a dark cloud on the horizon. That dark cloud was the coast of France. I smiled at the thought. France. A far-off boat whistle sounded a low note, a sea gull answered three octaves higher, then a sailor walked by and I complained, "Hey, Tierney, what's the holdup?"

"We're waitin' for the harbor pilot to come aboard and steer us into port. What's the matter, you gettin' antsy?"

"Am I ever. If he doesn't get here pretty soon, I may dive in and swim ashore."

"Just a word of warning, sailor, when you do go ashore, watch out for those French girls."

"Why? What do you mean?"

"They might lead you astray."

"Really?"

"Don't say I didn't warn you." He turned and walked away.

My eyes returned to the dark cloud, but my thoughts were now focused on "those French girls." I was born during the first World War and as I grew up, I heard veterans tell of their war experiences. Sometimes they would speak of "those French Girls" and smile.

A loud boat whistle announced the arrival of the pilot boat. The harbor pilot came aboard and took over the wheel. As our freighter headed east, the dark cloud gradually became the coast of France, then out of the morning mist, the port of La Palice materialized.

Our ship was almost too large for the port's facilities. Our huge propeller churned up swirls of muddy water from the bottom of the harbor, but the pilot skillfully guided the *West Chatala* into her slip.

The port of La Palice was a disappointment; it was drab and commercial with cranes, warehouses, and ships. We had a load of phosphate in our hold, destined for a nearby fertilizer factory. This was not the romantic seaport I had envisioned. However, I was told that a short bus trip away was the historic city of La Rochelle, practically unchanged since the religious wars of France. In those days, La Rochelle was a stronghold of the Hugenots, or Protestants. Today it is a mecca for French tourists.

When the *S.S. West Chatala* was secured, I, too, became a tourist, eager to see the sights and hopeful that I might meet some lovely mademoiselle who could be my guide and interpreter, since I spoke no French. The bus driver, who spoke a little English, suggested that I begin my visit by walking through the park of La Rochelle. It was beautiful. Paths meandered through meadows, then disappeared into wooded areas. While strolling along these paths, my eyes met friendly eyes; my smile was returned, but when a conversation started, the budding friendship crumbled. The language barrier proved to be a fatal handicap.

I passed a miniature golf course, and since I had nothing better to do, I decided to try my skill at putting. I was amazed to discover the course was made of cement—it gave a new dimension to the game. When I completed my round of golf, I spoke to the owner who turned out to be an Englishman. What a delight to be able to communicate again. As we shared our common language, I complained that my inability to speak French was destroying all my social aspirations.

"Oh?" said Mr. Whitebrook, looking off to the left, "Do you see that lady sitting in the middle of that bench over there, the brunette? She speaks English."

"Does she? Could you introduce me to her?"

He smiled. "I suppose I could. What's your name?"

"Terry O'Sullivan."

"An Irishman. I might have known. Come along."

Then with charm and ease he said, "Mademoiselle Doignon, I have a young friend here by the name of Terry O'Sullivan, who would like to meet you."

Mademoiselle Doignon smiled, stood up and offered me her hand. I was surprised by the strength in that hand.

I liked the way her black hair accented her blue eyes. She was medium height, not a beautiful woman; but she did have a charming smile and she

Historic port of La Rochelle

She took me to a quaint little restaurant and introduced me to eels in a yellow sauce. I hesitated—however, one taste overcame my Midwest provincialism. Claudine was easy to be with, and fun. I asked her the French word for park. She said "park."

I said, "No, Claudine, you misunderstand. I want to know the French word for park."

Again she said, "Park." I felt us being swept into the Abbott and Costello routine, "Who's on first?" Then she explained that park is spelled *parc* in French, but it sounds the same as p-a-r-k. Claudine was good company. She was quite poised and sure of herself. Our age difference apparently didn't matter.

A lovely summer evening was upon us and a stroll in the *parc* seemed the thing to do.

As we walked along, I said, "Claudine, I will always remember this day, thanks to you." She gave me a warm smile and quite spontaneously, I gave her a warm kiss. The kiss started the way most kisses start, but it did not finish the way most kisses finish. Mademoiselle Doignon was a lady of passion. In that first moment of togetherness it became apparent that we were destined to be lovers.

"Where shall we go?" panted I.

"Right here," panted she.

"But aren't we rather close to the path?"

"Darling, you're in France now."

Oui, so I was, and shortly thereafter, I was in Mademoiselle Doignon. Claudine was a lady of passion, far beyond anyone I had ever known. She so outdistanced me in this panting race of sexuality that I was left far behind. At one point, I had the feeling she was a marionette that I controlled. Finally, I caught up with my athletic mate and had my big moment. Then quiet returned to the *parc*. It was strange how we stimulated and fulfilled each other, but there was no togetherness. We were alone together pursuing our private fantasies. As I lay there in the grass, looking at the stars, I thought, "I will have to carry Claudine to her quarters." Wrong. Once on her feet, she seemed none the worse for wear and tear.

As we walked along, she broke the silence with "Charmant, you have such control for a young man."

I wanted to say, "It's because you are so far ahead of me that I can't catch up." However, I smiled and said, "You have such passion, Claudine. Much more than anyone I have ever known."

"Merci," said she, then that flirtatious smile.

My charming guide told me there was an island a few miles off the coast, the Ile De Ré. She asked if I would like to visit it tomorrow morning. "Oui!" So it was arranged that she would meet me in La Palice, where the *S.S. West Chatala* was tied up, and where we would board a boat for the Ile De Ré. She got on the bus with me to say good night, and I introduced her to our second mate, who was already aboard. She smiled and shook hands with him.

Then she turned to me and said, "Bon soir, Teree'. See you tomorrow."

She waved and got off the bus. The second mate said, "That woman's got a grip like a boiler maker."

I nodded and said, "That's not all she's got. Mademoiselle Claudine is one of a kind." Shortly thereafter I fell asleep, while visions of orgasms danced in my head.

Morning came and the shimmering perfection of a summer day made even the humble port of La Palice look pretty. I was sitting on a bench in the warm sun wondering if Claudine would be on the bus from La Rochelle. It occurred to me that I had no idea where she stayed, no phone number, no hotel. I was eager to make the voyage to the island, but I was also eager to make another voyage on the tempestuous sea of Mademoiselle Doignon's tireless hips. The bus pulled up and I watched as each person stepped off. Then, there she was. She stood there in the bright sunlight, looking poised and stylish.

"Bon soir, Claudine," I shouted as I approached her.

She smiled. "Non, Charmant, bon jour. Jour is day and soir is night."

So I sang, "Night and day, you are the one. Only you beneath the moon and under the sun." This delighted Claudine, so arm in arm we headed for the boat that would take us to the Ile de Ré.

On the boat, Claudine caught me staring at her. She said, "Why are you staring at me?"

I said, "Have you always lived in Paris?"

"No, I was born in Alsace-Lorraine, on a farm." Somehow, that didn't surprise me. She was of the earth, earthy and strong. A woman for all seasons. When we reached the island, the tide was out. There is a big difference between high and low tides in this area of France, and fat fishing boats lolled on their sides on the tidal shore. Fishermen were gathering shellfish. There were tidal pools where small eels tried unsuccessfully to hide under rocks. There were a couple of two-wheeled carts pulled by big draft horses, standing motionless, enhancing the seashore scenery. We watched for a few minutes, then caught a bus for the town of St. Martin. En route, we passed a barracks, where prisoners were held prior to being sent to Devil's Island, off the north coast of South America. So our bus driver informed us—translated, of course, by my charming guide and interpreter.

The town of St. Martin was unbelievably quaint; nothing had changed for centuries. During the French Revolution, street names had been changed, but some of the old names were still discernable. Claudine found all of this most fascinating; apparently she had looked forward to this visit for some time. We wandered through an ancient church. Generations of worshippers had given it a special aura. I professed a desire to see how the farmers lived, so we strolled out into the countryside and there in a pasture where cows grazed, lacking the camouflage my Catholic conscience would have appreciated, we made love. No, that isn't what we made; we made lust. "Some love is fire: some love is rust: but the purest, cleanest love is lust," so wrote Joseph Monecure March in his poem "The Wild Party."

Though I couldn't keep up with Claudine, the fires of her passion torched some of my inhibitions, and opened new vistas; and though I have lived a long and active life, I never again encountered such an oversexed lady as Mademoiselle Doignon.

As we wandered out of this overgrazed Garden of Eden, one cow slowly raised her head and stared at us with big, bulging eyes and parallel ears, then she returned to her grazing. I felt a kind of emptiness. What was it? Did I expect a round of applause?

We drifted back into town and stopped at a cafe which had a large stack of oyster shells near its entry, a practical way of advertising "Oysters on the Half Shell." This was another first for me. A taste of the sea, enhanced by lemon, sauce, crusty French bread and white wine.

Claudine said, "I'd like to take you back to Paris with me, Teree."

I said, "I'd really love to go to Paris with you, but I can't. I made a deal with my dad that makes it impossible. You see, I didn't want to go to college, so finally my dad said, 'If I can arrange a trip to Europe for you this summer, would you go to college for a year?' I said, 'If you can do that, I'll go to college.' That's how I got here, so now I've got to come through with my part of the bargain."

"But how was he able to get you on the ship, Teree?"

"He's a grain man and at one point in his career, he was involved in shipping wheat to Europe from Galveston, Texas. So he got to know some people in the Lykes Ripley Steamship Line."

Now she wanted to know how I spent my days aboard ship.

"In one word? I would say 'Painting!' But before you paint, you must chip the old paint off with a chipping hammer, then go after the rust spots with a steel brush, then repaint. Saltwater loves to eat metal, so the battle goes on forever. Then sometimes I steer the ship. Does that sound exciting? It isn't! You stare at a compass and try to hold your course on the designated number. If you start to daydream, the first mate will appear and say, 'What the hell's going on? Our wake looks like a snake.' Actually, I'm what they call a Work-a-way: a college student who works on the ship for $1.00 a month, but gets a free trip to Europe. We Work-a-ways are released as soon as we get to port. The regular seamen have to work their eight-hour day while in port. I'm free, so I can be with you, Claudine."

She smiled, and we wandered off, arm in arm.

We should have gone looking for another old church where we could say a few Hail Marys and repent, but we didn't. We were instead drawn to the ocean with its fresh breeze and the sound of surf. Then we spotted a gun emplacement which reminded us that peace is a gift to be enjoyed, and that love makes the world go round. The tall grass whispered and promised not to tell. We came together easily, then fell asleep. When we woke, the breeze had come up, as had the surf.

Claudine said, "Ou la la, let's get to zat boat, it won't wait. Alors!"

The return trip was a bit rough. I sang a song to Claudine which John, one of the sailors, had taught me. It seemed to sum up the way it is with sailors and their ladies:

> Every nice girl loves a sailor,
> Every nice girl loves a tar;
> For there is something about a sailor
> And you know what sailors are:
> Light and breezy, free and easy
> They're the ladies pride and joy;
> They fall in love with you and gin,
> Then they're off to sea again,
> Ship ahoy, Sailor boy.

When we reached La Palice, it was dark. I walked to the bus with Mademoiselle Doignon. We held hands and were silent as we walked along. We had been enormously close for two days. When we reached the bus, we had one of those lengthy French kisses. She said, "Au revoir, Teree."

"Au revoir, Claudine, I promise I won't forget you." And I never have.

2
To Be Enlightened

A SEA GULL GRACEFULLY WINGING his way over the blue ocean told us that land was just beyond the horizon. As we neared the end of our voyage, I knew that a sailor's life was not for me. It's a paradox; in a sense you live like a bird, skimming the ocean wave with no fences or barriers, but in reality you live in cramped quarters with a group of men that you work with, eat with, and sleep with. I love the ocean when I'm lying on the warm sand, listening to the rhythm of its surf, dreaming of faraway places.

Next day, the *S.S. West Chatala* tied up in Houston, Texas. The long voyage was over. Now I found my thoughts turning to college. I couldn't believe it, I, who had been a classical example of "the whining schoolboy…creeping like snail unwillingly to school," was now actually looking forward to college. Kansas City University was a new school in its second year of existence. It bore no resemblance to the oblong brick building with windows called Southwest High, which to my eye resembled a prison. K.C.U. was housed in an old stone mansion. The campus was spacious and tree-studded. It was a small, casual college with an ambience that appealed to me, and I became involved. It was here I learned that one of the great freedoms of this world is the human brain. The mind is boundless in its scope. The first trip to the moon was made in someone's mind. Here at K.C.U. I became involved in the process of learning. When grades came out, I received an A in psychology, B+ in public speaking, and the rest Cs.

As I looked at this rather impressive report card, my mind flashed back to my senior year at Southwest High. Saran Van Meter was my English teacher. She was a thin, energetic, bird-like lady who loved Byron, Keats, and Shelley. She adored William Shakespeare.

One day in June when I handed her my report card for my final grade, she looked at me with bright blue eyes and said, "Terry O'Sullivan, you great big beautiful boy, there just isn't anything you couldn't do if you put your mind to it, but I have to fail you. I'm sorry."

So saying, she printed the letter "F" on my report card, which, when added to my other poor grades, sank my ship. It took me five years to get through high school, but I finally made it.

Late one afternoon on the campus of K.C.U., I was having a chat with a coed. Casually, I asked, "What are you up to?"

She replied, "I'm going down to read for the play. Want to come along?"

Hesitating for a moment, I said, "Well, yeah! Why not?"

So off we went to the audition. The play was a murder mystery, *The Thirteenth Chair*. Auditions were being held by Blair Davies, the director, and—much to my surprise—I got a part. Isn't it amazing how a chance thing like asking a girl "What are you up to?" can change your whole life? I can understand how asking a girl "Will you marry me?" can change your life, but that's another chapter. Several chapters, actually. Meantime, back to *The Thirteenth Chair*.

Why did I so readily accept this invitation to read for a play? Perhaps my new attitude toward school had something to do with it. In high school they put on school plays every year, but I never went to see one of them, let alone try out for a part. Now I was going to be an actor. What would it be like? This was my renaissance. I was looking, I was seeking, I wanted to learn. I had recently discovered poetry, and found that I loved it. Now I was about to discover acting. I was very excited. As I drove home that evening, I asked myself, what traits had I displayed when growing up that might indicate a potential performer? Well, I did like to make people laugh and a classroom is a kind of audience, ready, willing, and able to laugh if you toss in a bit of Irish wit.

For example, in the sixth grade, Miss Swenson gave us a rather interesting assignment. We were to trace our ancestry back to our roots and report to the class from whence we sprang. When the day for revealing our heritage came, we discovered we had a number of blue bloods in our class. In that rather ordinary looking group of students was a great-great-ever so great grandson of Lord Delaware. Anne Hayden, on her mother's side, descended from a southern plantation owner. Ward Whipple could trace his lineage back to the *Mayflower*.

Now it was my turn. I stood up and said, "My grandfather, Cornelius O'Sullivan, came from Ireland and he ran a saloon down at Ninth and Walnut."

Big laugh from fellow classmates. This was during Prohibition times, when the mere mention of whiskey was a bit shocking. When the laughter subsided, Miss Swenson ordered me to sit down. Okay, I anticipated that my grandfather's profession would have an impact on the class, but I was stating facts. He did come from Ireland and he did run a saloon at Ninth and Walnut. One of our neighbors summed it up rather well. She said, "Terry was probably the only kid in that class who told the truth."

Had Miss Swenson not ordered me to sit down, I might have gone on to say that Grandfather Cornelius died many years before I was even born. It seems he had an unfortunate habit—a shot of whiskey before breakfast for an eye opener. Followed by who knows how many more as the day wore on. Grandma Julia said she never saw Con drunk, but one can't help wondering if she ever saw him sober. Let us close the subject by saying "Cornelius was a gentleman drinker."

We had a picture of him. He was a handsome fellow with curly hair and an ascot tie with a diamond stickpin. I would love to have met him but alas, Cornelius O'Sullivan petrified his liver with daily tippling and departed this life in his mid fifties.

What other potential actor traits did I display? I was a pretty good imitator. Owls, roosters, and crows were duck soup for me, but I became famous among family and friends for my imitation of Father Kennedy giving his Sunday sermon. Father Kennedy was never meant to be a public speaker. I guess God has so many things to look after, a few mistakes like Father Kennedy on a podium are bound to happen. Thanks to my dad's insistence that my two sisters and I attend Mass every Sunday, I had the opportunity to study the good priest's performance week after week, year after year, until I perfected his every flaw, one of which was a slight speech impediment. I achieved this flaw by placing the tip of my tongue against my upper front teeth and holding it there as I delivered my sermon.

I was amazed when Timothy Aloysius, the devout Catholic, permitted me to do my impression of Father Kennedy for friends of the family. They thought it was hilarious. Only the other day my sister, Barbara, asked me if I could still do Father Kennedy. Alas, sixty-five years had come and gone since my last sermon. All I could remember was the punch line: "Cast this man into the exterior darkness, where there is weeping and where there is gnashing of teeth." Try reading this aloud with the tip of your tongue pressed up against your front teeth.

We now return you to *The Thirteenth Chair,* where rehearsals are going on apace. In the cast was an actress who stood head and shoulders above her fellow thespians. She was a pretty girl and she had class—she also had a boyfriend. Her name was Ruth Warrick. Perhaps you know her as Phoebe Tyler from the TV soap, *All My Children.*

When a cast comes together to do a show, it becomes a team, sometimes very close. Then, when the final curtain falls, we scatter and sometimes don't ever see each other again. This was not true with Ruth. I saw her years later on the screen when she played Orson Welles' wife in the movie *Citizen Kane.* Then more years went by, and in the late fifties we ran into each other in New York where we were both involved in soap opera. We got together for lunch and marveled at how fate weaves us in and out of this fabric called life.

During the run of *The Thirteenth Chair,* something exciting happened to me. I liked the feel of being out on that stage. I liked the people involved in theater. When it was over, I was able to answer that tired old question, "What do you want to be when you grow up, Terry?"

Answer, "I want to be an actor."

When I repeated those words to my father, I might as well have said, "I want to be a pimp." He didn't think it was a good idea. However, I had someone on my side—my mother! Amy was a good singer; not a professional, but an accomplished amateur.

Timothy Aloysius O'Sullivan was not a large man, five-foot-nine, slender build. But he was a formidable opponent. I remember once, when I was about ten, he had an argument with a man who was bigger and stronger than he. A boy judges an opponent by size and strength. I was surprised by the verbal attack he launched. I fully expected to see Mr. O get the hell knocked out of him, but he didn't, and he emerged victorious. When he became angry, his gray eyes would open wide so you could really see the whites. He was a handsome man with black, curly hair and light Irish skin.

Although my darling mother was on my side in the debate about acting, she was not a strong woman; she was basically a fun person with a good sense of humor. Not a match for the fighting Irishman when the whites of his eyes were showing. My dad was dead set against my becoming an actor. His dream was that one day I would become a grain man like himself, up on the trading floor of the Kansas City Board of Trade, selling wheat, corn, and oats by the carload. For years he had been trying to nudge me into the grain market. But the more I saw of it, the less interested I became. As an office boy, I found minimal excitement in taking bills of lading to the Atchison, Topeka, and Santa Fe railway office; nor did my pulse quicken when I took samples of wheat to the lab for protein analysis. Stamping envelopes was not nearly as much fun as playing post office, a game I had recently learned at Nancy Coon's birthday party.

Timothy Aloysius O'Sullivan, the grain man,
one-time president of the Kansas City Board of Trade

Then there was that summer I spent in western Kansas at a country elevator near Dodge City. The romance of Dodge City is purely historical, I can assure you. A country elevator is one of those gray structures that sticks up in the air and breaks the monotony of the great Western plains. Its purpose is to receive grain from farmers and load it into boxcars for shipping to market.

First, I got a charley horse from pushing boxcars into position for loading; then came the real fun—loading a boxcar with wheat. First I would cooper the car—that meant nailing sections of wood across the boxcar door openings, leaving enough room at the top so I could crawl in. Then I would insert a large hose, about a foot in diameter, into the boxcar, from which spewed a steady stream of wheat. At the beginning, I could load from the outside, but eventually I had to crawl inside, with dust mask and shovel, to distribute the load. The temperature inside the boxcar was like a sauna. As I shoveled the wheat, my shirtless torso dripped with perspiration. Then the dust would cling to my wet skin so that, when I emerged from the loaded boxcar, I looked as though I had fallen into a mudhole. What person in their right mind could love the grain business?

When the wheat harvest ended, I moved to a wheat ranch to learn the grain business from the ground up, literally, by plowing the good earth. This was accomplished with a tractor that had iron cleats in the rear wheels for traction. Before the days of tractor tires. I drove this monster round and round a half section of prairie, dragging a one-way. A one-way was a big iron contraption about fifteen feet wide, with huge discs that churned up the earth and plowed a fifteen-foot swath. When you plowed with the wind at your back, a cloud of dust would sweep over you. I had a picture taken of me standing beside my tractor.

When I showed it to Timothy Aloysius, the grain man, he said, "Who is that?"

I said, "That's me, your son, with a quarter of an inch of Kansas dust on my face."

What really dusted me off about this western Kansas summer was the fact that, years later, I learned that my dad had paid that wheat farmer to keep me on his farm; then the farmer turned around and extracted slave labor from me—starting at 5:30 A.M. First chore, feed the hogs. They got to eat breakfast before I did. My father really had an obsession with the work ethic and the virtues of honest toil. He wanted me to become a grain man. I wanted to be an actor.

My dad and I had reached an impasse and I didn't know what to do about it. Then I remembered another crisis time. When I was in the fifth grade, my life was made miserable by a bully named Clede Lentz. Clede was a year older than I. He was bigger and stronger. As time went by, he started teasing me and pushing me around. It seemed that the more I took, the more he had to give. One day, in desperation, I doubled up my fist, threw a punch into my tormenter's face, and a fight began. It was a mobile battle that went on for about six blocks. There were attacks, retreats, skirmishes, and reprisals. A number of schoolchildren watched this sporting event—at a safe distance. Among the spectators was Charlotte Thompson. Her dad was a grain man, too, so a complete account of this neighborhood brawl got back to T. A. O'Sullivan. I can't tell you how proud he was that his son had the courage to stand up and fight it out with a bully. The boxing match was a standoff, really, but as far as I was concerned, I won—big time—because Clede Lentz never laid a hand on me—ever again.

I reasoned that since my dad had such admiration for a person who will stand up and fight for his rights, perhaps if I confronted him—verbally—he would admire my courage and go along with my career plans. I waited for the right moment. One evening, he headed for the basement to check the furnace, and I followed him down. This was man talk and there were too many ladies upstairs.

I led off with, "Dad, you love the grain business, don't you?"

"Yes," he replied.

"Well, I feel the same way about acting. For the first time, I've found something that really interests me."

He countered with, "No! No son of mine is going to be an actor."

"Why not?"

"Because it's a very risky business and a good way to become a bum."

"I have no intention of becoming a bum. I'm going to be a successful actor."

"Terry, I can help you get started in the grain business and I know you'd be good at it."

Then anger boiled up in me and I blurted out, "I don't like the grain business. I don't like anything about the grain business. This is my life we're talking about, and I don't think you're being fair about it. You know what I think? I think you're a stubborn Irishman."

His eyes flashed white. I held my ground. Then he turned and stomped up the stairs. I stood there thinking, "Now what have I done? Why did I say that?"

It turned out that I had said the right thing. The next day we had a peace conference. This time my mother sat in, and it was decided that next year I would attend the Kansas City Conservatory of Music and study dramatics. My dad was a reasonable man. When he became convinced that I wanted acting one hundred per cent, he went along with it—not happily, but he went.

I had a friend named Bill Theiss, whose dad was also a grain man; he told me that in the early days of my acting career, he would ask my dad, "How's Terry doing?" Timothy Aloysius would just shake his head.

Then, a few years later, when my career got into gear, Mr. O came up to Bill on the trading floor and said, "Hi, Bill, did you see Terry last night?"

"No."

"He was on 'The Edward R. Murrow Show' doing a *Life Magazine* commercial."

This chapter began at Kansas City University, and it will end at K.C.U. During my year there I did not leave a legacy, but I did get a poem published in the school paper. Robert Burns wrote "To a Mouse." I wrote:

To a Keg

Old keg of oak, with hoops of steel;
Oh, many a time thou hast made me reel,
Oh, many a time have I troubled thee
For a drink of thy dark blue jubilee.
Yes, many a day when depressed I felt,
By thee, drab keg I often knelt,
To drain thee of thy contents sweet,
My spirits rise was very fleet.

Empty now, alone you lie
To bring me thoughts of days gone by,
Memories come as memories will,
Memories sweet and memories ill;
But wait, my keg, thy life's not done,
When grapes grow dark we'll have our fun.

When school closed for the summer, Timothy Aloysius, the nudger, said I should get a job. I responded to an ad in the *Kansas City Star* that offered great monetary rewards to a young man with sales ability. The product was Real Silk Hosiery. I was interviewed by Mr. Ortman, the sales manager, who hired me on the spot. Why not; the job was strictly commission. Mr.

Ortman was a balding, waist-expanding, glasses-wearing, never-at-a-loss-for-words six- footer.

Each morning Mr. Ortman would hold a sales meeting and attempt to pump some enthusiasm into his sales crew, then send us forth with a positive point of view. Here are the lyrics to a parody we used to sing in those meetings—to the melody of "The Dark Town Strutter's Ball":

Stepping down the street with my bag of samples,
Ringing every doorbell that I see,
Now hear them shout with glee,
When they see those miles of styles I'm showing;
Keeps me busy writing down the colors.
Can't take orders fast enough.
Do they dance on all their toes,
When they see those Real Silk Hose,
They buy all they can
From the Real Silk Hosiery man.

Sorry, ladies, about the use of Real Silk Hosiery "man." You see, it rhymes with "can." The only thing that rhymes with "person" is "cursin." Let's see, we could sing…

They never stop cursin'
The Real Silk Hosiery person.

I'll admit it's closer to the truth, but it does take us into the realm of negativism and Mr. Ortman would never permit that.

Nor would Mr. Ortman have permitted the verbal battle that erupted in the Real Silk office one sweltering summer day, but alas, Mr. Ortman was not present to intercede when John Beaver accused Jean Frost of stealing one of his good customers. He implied she had lured his customer away with her womanly wiles. That did it! Jean exploded. I had never seen an argument between a man and a woman escalate to such heights of fury. I really thought they were going to square off and exchange blows. I was about to intercede when the door opened and Mr. Ortman strode in. The shouting stopped immediately. I suspect the combatants were relieved to see the big boss. He invited them into his office and a peace treaty was worked out behind closed doors.

My parents got along with each other. Yes, they had disagreements, of course, but never, ever anything that resembled the fracas I had just witnessed. It was an eye opener for me.

There was one segment of selling Real Silk Hosiery that I rather enjoyed. Part of our personalized service entailed measuring the length of m'lady's calf for knee-length hosiery. I had a tape measure attached to a little gizmo that slipped under the arch. Most of my customers seemed to enjoy having a young man kneeling before them to perform a personalized service, but a few super-shys quickly said, "Never mind; I'll do that myself."

After a summer of "Knock, knock, anybody home?" I looked forward to the first day of school with ill-concealed impatience, and finally that September day arrived.

3

Possum for Dinner? You Gotta Be Kiddin!

*B*EFORE WE PROCEED FURTHER, I must clarify something; Timothy Aloysius O'Sullivan was my dad's birth-certificate name. His nickname was Ted. That's what everybody called him—except me. I called him Timothy Aloysius, but that name was used only between me, myself, and I. The poetic cadence of Timothy Aloysius O'Sullivan caught my fancy. Howsomever, when he lectured me for failing to mow the lawn or perform some other dreary chore, I called him Tyrannical Tim. This name, too, was confined to the ego trio. I wouldn't dream of verbalizing Tyrannical Tim! Are you kidding?

Here I must relate an incident that shows Timothy Aloysius O'Sullivan in one of his finer moments. When I was a lad of twelve, I thought of myself as the great white hunter. I could step out the front door armed with my shotgun, walk three blocks, and start hunting. I was also a trapper: muskrats, skunks, and possums were trapped and skinned, their pelts put on stretcher boards to dry, then sold to a fur buyer.

My mother once said, "Terry, you should be a surgeon."

I asked "Why?"

She said, "Because you always have blood on your hands."

I had heard that baked possum was a culinary delicacy, so naturally I wanted to try it. I often gave possum carcasses to Veenie, a delightful black lady who came to our house every Thursday to wash our clothes. I arranged to have Veenie instruct me in the art of possum baking. I had trapped a big one, skinned him, put his pelt on a stretcher board, then hung his carcass out on the back porch to freeze.

Possoms are strange little animals. For one thing, they are marsupials—they carry their young in a pouch, like a kangaroo. They have a rat-

21

Possum for dinner?
1928

like tail, small leather ears, a pointed face, beady little eyes, and front paws somewhat like a person's hands. They are about the size of a very small dog. Also they show their teeth when stressed, but it looks as if they are smiling.

Possums are relatively defenseless, rather slow and awkward of gait. Hopefully they can get to a tree and climb it to elude their foes. If caught on the ground, they feign death. Hence the expression "playing possum." They do have one redeeming feature: a light-gray, long-haired fur coat. But this asset adds man to their list of enemies.

I learned from Veenie that baking possum is much like baking a chicken or a roast. Along with the aforementioned entree, we would have candied sweet potatoes and black-eyed peas. Veenie seemed to get a kick out of instructing me in the art of baking a possum.

Once while skimming excess fat from the baking possum, I thought to myself, "This damn thing looks like a small dog." I quickly put that thought out of my mind and concentrated on my cooking.

When 'twas time for the evening meal, there was an air of expectancy in our household. This was going to be a big surprise for Timothy Aloysius. My dad's mother was staying with us at this time, so with Grandma and my two sisters, Barbara and Kathleen, we had a family gathering of six around the dining-room table. At the appropriate moment, I proudly brought the baked possum in on a carving platter and placed it in front of the gentleman at the head of the table. A heavy silence fell.

Finally himself broke that silence with an ominous question, "What the hell is this?"

I proudly chirped up, "That's baked possum."

He stared at me with disbelieving gray eyes and said, "Do you mean to tell me this is that thing I've seen hanging on the back porch every morning when I went to work?"

I nodded.

He stood up and said, "Aim, get your coat. We're going out to dinner."

And out the door they went. I assumed head-of-the-table position and served. Actually, the possum wasn't bad. It tastes a bit like fat pork. I do wish it hadn't looked like a small dog, but dammit, it really did!

4
April Love

*G*EORGE PHELPS WAS OUR INSTRUCTOR in the drama department at the Kansas City Conservatory of Music. He was a small man with an inexhaustible flow of vitality and a good sense of humor. Early on it was discovered that I dropped the letter "g" in the "ing" family. I said "goin'", "comin'." Mr. Phelps, assisted by my fellow students, would stop me any time I failed to attach that final "g," so I got over that omission in a relatively short time.

One day I did my impression of Father Kennedy, and that gave me a little standing in the theatrical community. We studied voice, body movement, and pantomime, and we did scenes from plays. I loved the curriculum. It seemed more like play than work.

The artistic bent in our family came from my mother. She had a beautiful dramatic soprano voice. She loved books and poetry. Her uncle, Jacob Nesch, was a professional painter who practiced his art in Switzerland. Some of his paintings still hang in the town hall in the village of Balgach in northeast Switzerland.

My sister, Barbara, two years younger than I, was a good dancer. She had studied tap since she was a wee one, and later became a professional dancer. At this time, however, it had been suggested that she study ballet, so she went to a well known ballet instructor named Dorothy Perkins.

One day I drove Barbara to her dance lesson, and rather than wait in the car, I joined her. Barbara introduced me to Miss Perkins. I told the lady that I was a drama student and asked if I might watch the class. She seemed delighted to have me. Miss Perkins was working with two groups, beginners and advanced students. In the advanced group was a darling little ballerina, more precise in her movements than her classmates, a cute figure, her hair bleached white like Jean Harlow's, blue eyes and a laugh that rippled.

"Who is that?" I asked Miss Perkins.

"Her name is Norma Jayne Duncan. She's one of my most talented students."

About halfway through the class, Norma Jayne's mother arrived. She sat down beside me to watch. We introduced ourselves. She seemed eager to talk about her daughter. I learned that Norma was an only child and the focal point of her life. Mrs. Duncan was definitely a career mother, dreaming of stardom for Norma and reflected glory for herself. We watched the dancers; *plié, entrechat,* and *tour jeté.*

I had always been interested in dancing, but that day I fell in love with it. I couldn't take my eyes off Norma Jayne. After the class, I told Miss Perkins that I would like to study with her, and she said she would be delighted to have me as a student.

As time went by, Norma and I became friends. I asked her if we could go dancing some weekend. She said she'd love to. So one Friday night we went to the Plamore Ballroom, where Ted Fiorito and his orchestra were playing. Norma and I danced beautifully together. She seemed to anticipate my every move as we glided across the floor.

I treasure the memory of the "Big Band Era." The lyrics of their songs were romantic and the music was dreamy and danceable. Our first date turned out to be a perfect evening. Norma and I started dating.

There were nights when we parked in the dark—to kiss and whisper. Just two blocks from my home was a wonderful "park in the dark area." A developer had put in the streets, but hardly anyone came to buy lots or build houses, so those dark, empty streets became our Lover's Lane. The west side of this development was bounded by an Osage orange hedge and a mockingbird would sing there at night. Norma's white hair looked beautiful in the moonlight.

One night I said, "Norma, I think I'm falling in love with you. I've been going with girls since I was fifteen, but I never felt like this. I can't really explain how it is, I only know it feels wonderful."

Then Norma said, "I feel the same way about you, Terry."

The wanting to be with, the longing to possess, it all flowed so naturally, until we did possess each other, with love. That is more than a glimpse of paradise. It seemed to me there was just the two of us in a beautiful, moonlit world. At night I would dream of Norma. When I woke, she would invade my thoughts.

Early Visitor

The instant that I woke this morning,
A door in my mind quickly opened
And you stood there smiling;
Then you walked in, with all your charm
To spend the day in my thoughts.

There were other poems, forgettable and forgotten, but this one was neither of the above.

Life Has No Mystery

The silent strength and beauty of nature
Seen by the light of a cloud-draped moon;
Life has no mystery,
We care not why we're here;
To be here is enough, Beloved,
It will end soon.

When I wrote that poem, I had no feeling of impending doom. Strange about writing. Sometimes it goes where it wants to go, and says what it wants to say. The writer merely moves his pen along the page.

We were in love. I thought we would always be together. I was twenty, Norma was sixteen. Romeo and Juliet. And like Romeo and Juliet, tragedy was waiting up ahead. Norma missed her period. How could this happen? We were so careful, but as the days went by, we began to panic. Truly we were babes in the woods. I suggested that maybe we should get married. We were in love and there didn't seem to be many options. So it was decided that if she missed her next period, we would get married, secretly. Meantime, I would set about preparing for the event, just in case. The deadline passed. One evening, my cousin, Bobby Nesch, and my sister, Barbara, joined us at the preacher's to witness the marriage ceremony. One week after our marriage, Norma had her period.

Norma's behavior had alerted her parents to the fact that something was wrong with their only daughter. Under heavy grilling, Norma burst into tears and told her parents we were married. And then did all hell break loose. Daddy Duncan threatened to shoot me. Most fathers with betrayed daughters threaten to shoot the seducer if he doesn't marry their daughter.

I was threatened because I had. Mother Duncan, however, was the one who really read me the riot act. She screamingly accused me of marrying Norma because I knew that her daughter was destined to be a movie star and I wanted to go along for the ride.

Those words really seared my soul. They became a part of me, like Hester Prynne's scarlet letter. I swore that I would show this lady that however far her daughter went in show business, I would go farther. Her words became a spur in my side, goading me ever onward and upward. Nor did I ever forget her words.

My parents were great in this crisis. If they had come down on me with both feet, I don't know what I'd have done. I guess they could see that I was suffering. And I truly was.

The marriage was annulled. I was heartbroken. Mrs. Duncan took Norma Jayne out to Hollywood where she thought the movie industry would quickly recognize her daughter's talent and make a movie star out of her—the Hollywood fantasy. Norma did a couple of bit parts and some extra work, then married a wine merchant and joined the vast parade of humanity that marches ever onward, unknown and unsung.

My irreplaceable love, Norma Jayne, was gone. All I had left was a growing determination to make it in show biz. How? By working at it. Timothy Aloysius had taught me that if you want something, you work for it. So I went to work.

5

In the Big Tent Theater

*I*LEARNED THAT MY OLD HOME TOWN, K.C. MO, was the booking head-quarters for Midwest Tent Shows. This was not Chautauqua, but legit-imate theater, presented in a big tent—120 feet long by 80 feet wide. These shows traveled through the Midwest during the summer months, playing county fairs and one-week stands in small towns.

I called on Ken Wayne, a theatrical agent. Mr. Wayne told me that the Original McOwen Players, headquartered in Topeka, Kansas, were look-ing for a young leading man. He said that if he could set up an audition for me, he would drive me out there. The following weekend we drove to Topeka, Kansas. I read for Mrs. McOwen and her director, Bill Trout, and got the job. My first professional acting job! What a thrill!

I didn't know it at the time, but I got in on the end of an era. This was 1936 and tent shows were headed for oblivion. Movie theaters were begin-ning to appear in small country towns. However, on this particular spring day, the McOwen Players were looking forward to a prosperous summer in northeast Kansas and eastern Nebraska.

I tried to appear calm and professional as I checked into Hotel Throop, Topeka, Kansas. My fellow actors called it "Hotel Throwup, Tah-puke-ah, Kansas." It was a bit seedy and old fashioned. Most nights a bat would go swooping up and down the high-ceilinged hallways. "They were catching mosquitoes," or so I was told. That's like telling me that Frankenstein makes big charitable contributions. When I was a boy, the kids in my neighborhood told me that a bat could dive bomb you and get tangled up in your hair. As a lad, I had pictured in my mind what that catastrophe could be like. The bat would be screeching, as distressed bats do, his white teeth gleaming, his leathery wings beating frantically on my scalp. I wouldn't dare put my hand up there to knock him off, because the bat would bite it. Then I'd get hydrophobia. Hydrophobia makes you foam at the mouth. When I walked the dimly lit halls of Hotel Throwup, I did so with my fingers tightly locked over my head. Do you blame me?

I saw very little of Tapukah, Kansas, but I saw a great deal of that hotel. I had six plays to learn almost immediately, if not sooner. Fortunately, I was blessed with a good memory, and since the other actors lived down the hall or up on the next floor, I could usually find someone to give me my cues. Even so, it was a monumental task, like cramming for finals.

As though that weren't enough, I then discovered that a tent show actor was expected to do a specialty number—like sing, dance, play an instrument, or do a magic act. I mentioned that I could sing a little, so they auditioned me and said, "Yes, you do sing a little—a little off-key. But on your credits you stated you had been a Real Silk hosiery salesman. I think we have a job for you! We need a pitchman for our candy sales."

And that became my specialty: pitchman for the candy sale.

The Candy Man gambit went like this. When the curtain closed at the end of the first act, I would step out on the apron and say:

"Good evening, ladies and gentlemen. This box which I am holding is full of delicious candy. Sound good? Let me assure you, it is. The manufacturers of this candy wanted us to introduce their product to your community, so we are able to offer it to you at a very special price—just 25¢ a box. Each box contains ten pieces of delicious candy. But that's not all. Many of these boxes contain coupons redeemable for these beautiful prizes."

The curtain would open revealing a display of "flash"—show biz jargon for prizes, such as sparkling rayon bedspreads, standing lamps, and table lamps. When the "Oh's" and "Ah's" subsided, I would continue.

"Once in a great while, you are offered an opportunity where you cannot lose. For your quarter, you will receive 25¢ worth of delicious candy, plus a good chance of winning one of these beautiful prizes. Have your quarter ready. The boys are coming down the aisles. Music, maestro, please!"

The orchestra would strike up a lively tune and the candy sale would begin.

You all know by now that there isn't really a Santa Claus, so I will reveal the inner workings of our candy sale. The boxes of candy which contained "coupons" redeemable for prizes were plainly marked. These were called ballys. The canvas crew salesmen were instructed to hand out ballys generously at first, to get winners on their feet and walking up to the stage. When a coupon was handed to me, I would read off the number loud and clear. The number meant nothing. I controlled the gift giving. My objective, to stimulate sales. Early on, a couple of big prizes would be handed out. When I had a number of winners stacked up in front of the stage, I would hand out some incense, then a hot water bottle (held on high for a laugh), then a floor lamp if sales were beginning to slack off. We sold a lot of candy and everyone had a lot of fun.

Earl and Joey Gregg had a delightful specialty number. When the curtain opened, they were discovered center stage, looking just like an old-fashioned daguerreotype photo; she seated, he standing beside her, his hand on her shoulder. They were dressed in costumes from the early 1900s. When the applause faded, they would sing:

We're gonna have our tintypes taken,
We're gonna have our picture took,
Gonna send them away to the folks back home
And show them how we look.
We used to be small time fellers,
But now we know the book;
We've been everywhere,
We've seen everything,
So we're gonna have our tintypes took.

Then they would glide into a soft shoe number that ended with their returning to their original tableau. A hard act to follow.

The McOwen Sisters were accomplished hoofers. They combined dance with song for a musical interlude that was an audience pleaser. I thought the Original McOwen Players gave their audiences a lot of entertainment for the price of a ticket.

We opened our season in Beatrice, Nebraska. Opening week had gone well, and now it was Saturday night. Our play was *Steppin' Sisters*, a fast-paced farce. As with most farces, there is that final scene where a rather bizarre plot gets resolved. Earl Grey, our character man, was delivering an emotional tirade, finger pointed at Lance Davis—when he came forth with a beautiful spoonerism.

He shouted, "You've wooled the pull over my eyes—till..." Audience and cast froze for an awkward moment. Then Lance tried to reply, but he couldn't. He turned upstage, shaking noticeably, and the breakup began—audience and cast in waves of laughter! So, for the rest of the season, every Saturday night in every town, Earl would point his finger at Lance and say, "You've wooled the pull over my eyes—till..." Lance would turn upstage, the audience would start to laugh, and the cast would collapse, just as though it were happening for the first time. Well, why not? We were there to make people laugh, and we did!

Steppin' Sisters should have been named *Stumblin' Sisters.* As the season went on, it became notorious for late entrances, forgotten props, and speeches paraphrased in the damnedest ways. Thespis, the Greek god of drama, had placed a curse on our favorite farce. But no matter what we did, the audience laughed and seemed to love it.

One night, Elton Hackett and I were zipping through some clever dialogue, seated at a table. Out of the corner of his mouth, in a whisper, he hissed four fatal words, "Your fly is open."

Oh, my God! Could he be kidding? No, he wasn't. My fly was definitely open. A moment ago I had been so poised and debonair. Now I was shattered and exposed in front of hundreds of people. The actor's nightmare was my reality. Why do actors make such a monstrous thing out of a little faux pas like this? I don't know why, but we do. We constantly change costumes in a hurry. It's inevitable that some day a zipper will remain unzipped. Burlesque comedians run around the stage with their shirt tail hanging out through their fly, or pin a padlock on same for safekeeping, but we legitimate actors become utterly apoplectic when someone whispers, "Your fly is open."

Meantime, lines are being said, or partly said, or tossed out the window. "The window," I thought. "That's it. I'll go look out the upstage window and zip that mother up." Which I did, blushing through my stage makeup. To my surprise, the world continued to spin and the play went on. But do remember, this was my first professional job and my whole career seemed ready to topple in that awful moment. It was such a shock that I have literally spent the rest of my life checking my fly. Should you observe me doing so, please remember it's not an obscene gesture; it's just a permanent tic.

The average person works Monday through Friday and has the weekend off, but the canvas crew of a tent show reverses this work formula. Even before the final applause has died for the Saturday night show, they start grabbing things. Theirs is a monumental task. The expression, "pull up stakes and go" must have originated with tent shows. Every stake the crew had rhythmically pounded into the earth with sledgehammers must now be pulled up and loaded on trucks. *Everything* must be loaded on trucks. The stage, the props, seats, canvas, even the popcorn machine, then driven to the next town. Upon arrival, the crew might catch a short nap and start the hellish task of putting it all back together again—in time for the

Monday night performance. If the distance between the two towns was considerable, they might do a complete reversal of the work week, by working their full forty hours on an extended weekend. Not recommended for the faint of heart.

That first summer in the big tent theater was not easy. I was new to the business and there was much to learn. Also, I missed Norma Jayne. The expression "heartache" is an accurate description of what I felt. I consoled myself with the thought that when this show ended, I would go to California and find my lost love. But when the show did end, I wavered. I asked my parents what they thought. They felt it would be the wrong move. Maybe later, but not now. They felt I should accept the scholarship I had been offered at the Irvine School of Drama in New York City. Meantime, I phoned my agent and made an appointment.

6

The J. Mickey O'Brien Players
of Carthage Junction, Tennessee

T HE ONLY JOB that Ken Wayne could offer me was one that he, admittedly, knew nothing about, and about which he could therefore make no guarantees. However, the name fascinated me: the J. Mickey O'Brien Players of Carthage Junction, Tennessee. That sounded like an adventure to me, and an O'Sullivan should be able to get along with an O'Brien. So I repacked my wardrobe trunk and headed for the hills.

The train trip was delightful. The wooded hills of Tennessee reminded me of the Ozark Mountains in southern Missouri, where I often vacationed during my growing-up years. The hills and the people who inhabit them have always attracted me. Hillside farming does not produce wealthy farmers, but it does turn out a resilient breed of men who manage, by hook or crook, to wrest a living from the land. In the hook department are hunters, fishermen, and tie hackers. The latter are woodsmen who convert logs into railroad ties with an axe, an adz, and lots of muscle. In the crook category you might find a few stills, hidden somewhere off in the distant hills, that are capable of converting kernels of corn into moonshine whiskey. Bottled and sold in mason jars, it looks just like water, but have a care, this is firewater and it kicks like a Missouri mule.

My musing was interrupted by the conductor calling out, "Carthage Junction, next stop, Carthage Junction."

I was the only traveler that got off at Carthage Junction. Standing on the platform was a small man. He approached me smiling, with hand extended.

"You must be Terry, I'm Mickey. Welcome to Carthage."

My agent told me that J. Mickey was a Toby comedian. This was a creature that was spawned by, and flourished in, Midwest tent shows, a kind of Peck's Bad Boy, second cousin to a circus clown, whose makeup consisted of freckles, a red wig, and a blacked out tooth. His objective was to get the laugh—at any cost.

J. Mickey was a loquacious fellow, and as we drove from Carthage Junction to Carthage proper, he told me of his plans. Ours was to be a circle stock company. Carthage would be our base or hub. Each Tuesday night we would open a new play in Carthage. On Wednesday we would drive to Temperance Hall and give a performance; on Thursday nights we played Difficult; on Friday, Defeated. Here I had to interrupt. I thought he was kidding me about the names of these towns.

"No," he said, "these towns received their names during the Civil War."

When we arrived at Carthage we went straight to J. Mickey's mobile home where I was introduced to the rest of the company: Mickey's wife, Lynn, an attractive lady, much younger than he; their daughter, Mary, about nine years old; and Blair Davis and his wife Ginny. This twosome had served some time in burlesque. Ginny's face was a bit tired, but her body was remarkably intact. Blair was a character man in his fifties.

J. Mickey said, "We might as well do a read-through since we're all here."

So saying, he passed out parts for a play called *Sputters, the Stutterin' Cowboy.* That title should tell you a great deal about our opening play. In two words: low comedy. Sputters was played by J. Mickey himself in the Toby tradition—broad. I played Ramon, a villainous Mexican, who said things like, "Wan, two more treeps cross bordair and I see deese accursed Gringos no more. I no trade one drop my blood for all Gringo blood on earth."

You marvel that I can still remember those lines? I keep hoping that some day I'll forget them.

After the read-through, J. Mickey, assisted by Lynn, told us how they had made their living the past few years. It was a real gypsy life. They lived in a trailer home with their nine-year-old daughter. Their game was to go to a small town and spread the word that there would be a free show in town tomorrow night. The news would spread through the hills like wildfire. Farm families would drop whatever they were doing and head to town for a free show.

J. Mickey had a vast collection of jokes, skits, bits, and blackouts. Mickey did stand-up comedy, then he and Lynn did comedy skits. They even involved their daughter in some of their skits. How did they make a living? From the proceeds of the candy sale. The reason they formed this stock company was so they could have a permanent residence and send their daughter to school.

J. Mickey should have heeded the names of those Tennessee towns, Difficult and Defeated. These words foretold our fate. It really wasn't a very good production. Although people would flock to town to see a free show, they stayed away in droves when it came to paying admission. For an actor it's depressing to be playing comedy that isn't getting laughs. It seemed the harder we tried, the worse it got. The most inadequate facility we played in was a schoolhouse that could be converted into a town hall or theater. Picture a stage where the curtain is a flimsy cloth hung on a wire with safety pins. Someone had to walk it open and someone had to walk it closed. The backing was only six feet high, which meant that if I walked from left stage to center to make an entrance, my cowboy hat would seem to float on top of the backing. So I had to crouch down as I walked, then stand erect when I got to center stage.

Once when Blair and I were putting on our makeup by the light of a kerosene lamp, he paused, looked over at me and said, "Well, kid, I guess the next stop will be the shit house."

Yes, it did seem that we were scraping the bottom of the show-biz barrel. J. Mickey had no money. When the first week was a fiasco, he folded. So one bright October morning, J. Mickey drove me to the highway. The Cumberland River looked beautiful as it flowed by, and the leaves were starting to turn. We got out of his car. I thanked him and wished him luck. We shook hands. He said, "Terry, I've got a hunch that you're gonna make it." Then he got back into his car, waved, and drove away. I treasured those words, for it felt very lonely standing there with my suitcase by my side and not a car in sight. I wondered what Norma Jayne was doing. She had to be doing better than this.

Finally a car stopped. I hopped in beside a farmer. He was a friendly fellow, eager to talk. I asked him how they managed to plow the hillsides the way they do. He told me they had hillside plows. When they got to the end of a row, they would flip the plow around so it threw the earth in the same direction when you went back in the opposite direction.

My friendly farmer gave me a thirty-mile ride and left me in the middle of nowhere, surrounded by hills and trees. There I stood for quite a spell, wondering how long this journey might take. A maroon car came around the bend. As it passed, I could see it had Massachusetts license plates, so I shouted out "New York!" The car drove on, then stopped. I broke into a run. The man was headed for New York City. I couldn't believe my good fortune. We took turns driving and made the journey nonstop.

7

New York, New York

THE HOLLAND TUNNEL, which runs under the Hudson River, is an exciting introduction to New York City. Bumper-to-bumper traffic flows through this shimmering tube of bright lights and gleaming tiles, with imposing policemen on scaffold walks along the sides. Even so, I was not prepared for what burst forth on the other side. People, cars, skyscrapers: it honked, it hurried, it pulsated. Where were they all going, these swarms of people, stepping briskly as though they were five minutes late? I was the only one who didn't have a destination. I stood there, bewildered, suitcase in hand. A stranger in a foreign land, fascinated and overwhelmed.

In all this vast metropolis with its teeming millions, I had only two contacts. Number one, the Irvine School of Drama, where I had been offered a scholarship. Contact number two was an aspiring actress, Peggy Adams, whom I had met at the Kansas City Civic Theater.

Contact number two became phone call number one. In our conversation, she talked about Mike, her boyfriend, and invited me to join them for dinner. We went to a Chinese restaurant called "Shanghi," which featured complete meals for twenty-five cents. Yes, from egg-drop soup to fortune cookies, only twenty-five cents. Even so, actors sometimes had trouble coming up with a quarter. This was 1936.

Mike, a Kansas Citian, was performing at the Cherry Lane Theater in Greenwich Village. This was an off-Broadway theater, owned and operated by an older actor, Mr. Gilmore. He chose plays that had parts for himself and his daughter, Virginia. His current show, *Accent on Youth* was typical. Older Writer is enamored of his Secretary; Secretary is attracted to Older Writer, but is lured away by Young Football Player. In the end, she returns to the security and sanity of older actor.

Actors received no pay at the Cherry Lane, but were provided a show-case where they could invite agents and producers. Also, Mr. Gilmore cast two or three actors in each role, so if someone couldn't make a scheduled performance, there was a backup available.

Mike told me that Mr. Gilmore was looking for an actor to play Dickie, the Football Player. He thought I might be right for the part, so the next evening I joined Mike on his trip to the Cherry Lane Theater. The trip was unforgettable. We descended a flight of stairs to the underground world of subway trains. We each put a nickel in the slot, passed through the turnstile, and joined the crowd waiting on the platform. Suddenly the thunderous subway train exploded into the station. The moment it stopped, the door slid open and a flood of humans poured out, only to be replaced by another bustling horde eager to find a seat. It seemed to me there was a pervasive urgency to New Yorkers. I wondered if I would be able to fit into this alien land. I felt like a tourist from Podunk, but I was eager to learn.

Accent on Youth was a good play, and the part of Dickie seemed a nat-ural for me. After the performance, I was able to read for Mr. Gilmore.

Meantime, I found a small room on East 52nd Street for $2.50 a week. The bathroom was down the hall. The room was long and narrow, like a walk-in closet with a door at one end and a window at the other. It was so narrow that I had to leave my wardrobe trunk open in order to get past it.

The people at the Irvine School loved my story of the J. Mickey O'Brien Players of Carthage Junction, Tennessee, and agreed to take me on. Why did a school of drama offer scholarships to young men? Because in those days more women than men were interested in studying dramat-ics. So to keep a balance in their enrollment, they offered a few scholar-ships to young men. We studied voice and diction, worked on scenes, took dance lessons twice a week, and had a class in fencing. The dance class was conducted by Edwin Strawbridge. He could see that I had some back-ground in dance and wanted to know where I had studied. I told him I had worked with Dorothy Perkins in Kansas City, and that a couple of her stu-dents had managed to get jobs in New York at Radio City Music Hall.

Three weeks after my audition at the Cherry Lane, Mr. Gilmore tele-phoned. He wanted me to start rehearsal immediately, and to perform Sunday and Thursday nights. Rehearsals were scheduled in the daytime, which conflicted with school. Also at this point in my life, I had a prob-lem that was to plague me the remainder of my days: a shortage of bills in my billfold.

I could have written Timothy Aloysius about my brilliant future that was being threatened by a lack of wherewithal, or I could drop out of school and find a job. I chose the latter. Once again, I apologized to the people at Irvine School. Mr. Strawbridge asked for my phone number and said there could be something in a month or so. I wanted to know what that something was.

He said, "If it happens, I'll call you."

"Okay, thanks, Mr. Strawbridge. I look forward to hearing from you."

I needed a job. One of my fellow actors at the Cherry Lane told me that on Sixth Avenue there were employment agencies. They put job descriptions on cards and displayed them outside their offices. Since I had no skills, I decided a restaurant job might be best. At least I'd have food to eat. I got a job at McCowan's Restaurant in Queens Plaza, Long Island.

Actually, McCowan's was a bar, a restaurant, and a soda fountain. I was paid ten dollars a week plus food. The irony of it was that the more I worked with food, the less interest I had in eating it. No reflection on McCowan's menu, just one of those tricks the fates play on us. Instead of having Hungarian goulash and noodles, the Blue Plate Special, I would scramble some eggs for myself, or make a malt.

I worked wherever they needed me, but mostly in the soda fountain, which did a good lunch business. Everyone arrived at five minutes past noon and left at five minutes before one. It was sheer pandemonium. Everything was on the double. More than once I threw a tea bag into a cup and then poured coffee on it.

My boss, Al, was a small guy, but he compensated for his size with his Brooklyn toughness. One day he looked over my shoulder when I was putting together a chocolate soda.

"What the hell are you doing?" he asked.

"Making a chocolate soda," I replied.

"Who told you to do it that way?"

"That's the way we make them in Kansas City. This way makes a better soda."

"I don't give a damn about better soda! You make 'em the way we make 'em or you'll find your ass out in the street."

This was truly a cultural shock for me. I had been brought up to do everything the best way I knew how. Now here was a man saying, "We're not interested in the best way. Our way is good enough. Do it our way or get the hell out of here."

"Okay, Al."

He had delivered his lines like George Raft reading the riot act to a rival gangster. I was convinced. Henceforth, I made sodas the McCowan way, chintzy. But when I made a chocolate soda for myself, I made it the K.C. way. With lots of ice cream. The way God intended it to be.

The speeding, thundering subway trains flashing by like cans of sardines no longer caused my head to turn. One day I was able to direct a lady to her destination. I said to myself, "Hey, I'm becoming a New Yorker." I remember standing in Grand Central Station one evening, amazed by the number of people rushing past me. I thought, this swarm of humanity that resembles an active ant colony is made up of individuals, each one with a long list of needs: money, career, recognition, love.

I was rather proud of myself. Six weeks ago I had been standing on a corner with a suitcase, overwhelmed by the tempo and size of Manhattan. Now I had a job, a room, and a part in a play. But the winds of change were blowing again. I received a call from Mr. Strawbridge. Would I be interested in a three months' tour?

"Would I be interested? When do we leave?"

So it was arranged that I would audition for his partner on Thursday at 2:00 P.M. on East 14th Street. I wasn't prepared for this meeting. His partner was beautiful. Long black hair parted in the middle, a bun in the back, white skin, cool and poised. The body of a dancer. Thirties, early? Even her name was fascinating: Lisa Parnova. I had to go on this tour. I invited them to come to the Cherry Lane Theater to see me perform in *Accent on Youth*.

After I left the audition, my mind kept flashing back to Lisa Parnova, the beautiful ballerina. Then I said to myself, "Aw, come on, Terry. Let's not start dreaming the impossible dream. Women like that are always involved, and even if she weren't, forget it." But I couldn't forget it. Lisa Parnova. The name fit her perfectly. She was like a princess from a Russian novel.

A week later I was called back to 14th Street, this time to discuss terms. I would dance, drive a car, handle luggage, and help Tony with sets. But I would get to see Lisa every day.

Her halo became a bit crooked at times during those long days of tough rehearsal...and they were long and tough. I have always remembered one thing she told me: "If you make a mistake, don't convey it to the audience by gesture or facial expression. Keep your poise and the audience probably won't notice." Lisa had been a ballerina in Germany. What a beautiful dancer she was. "Hope springs eternal in the human heart." My dance partner, Ann, was a nice girl and I should have turned my attention to her, but I couldn't. I had fallen for Lisa, and although my chances of becoming the man in her life were exceedingly remote, I couldn't change my feelings. The cards had been dealt and the game had to be played, win, lose or draw.

Edwin Strawbridge had a good sense of humor. He was a small man, five-foot-seven, well-built, and an accomplished dancer. I, on the other hand, was tall, six-foot-one. This difference in height worked to our advantage in the choreography of "The Sorcerer's Apprentice." I, the evil sorcerer, danced behind my apprentice, Strawbridge, my fingers moving above his head as though he were a marionette that I controlled.

Finally that exciting day dawned. The start of the Strawbridge Parnova tour. The scenery truck, driven by Tony, had already headed for Connecticut. Hugo was to drive the Ford; I was assigned to drive the big Packard. My co-pilot was Lisa. Was the cool Russian Princess beginning to thaw? Maybe. There she sat, remarkably close, delightfully poised. She smiled at me and we headed north.

After a few miles, I casually asked, "You're not married, Lisa?"

She replied, "No. I was, but not anymore."

Our goal that morning was Hartford, Connecticut, but en route we were stopped for speeding. Thank God I wasn't in the lead. Apparently quite a few New Yorkers had failed to pay their speeding tickets in Connecticut, so the new approach was to haul them into the police station and collect the fine then and there. Lisa was not inclined to write a check for the stated amount, so dickering ensued. Dickering that culminated with Lisa walking out, leaving Hugo and me, the two drivers, to wonder what our fate might be. Our suspense was short lived.

An officer said, "Okay, boys, follow me." This we obediently did, down the stairs and into a cell. We couldn't believe this was happening. When the officer left, we broke out laughing. It was noon, so we figured the rest of our company would go to lunch, then would come back and bail us out. I played Gepetto, the woodcarver, and Hugo Fiorato played the violin. As far as we were concerned, this incarceration was a lark. They had to bail us out—we had a show to do.

Our friendly jailer arrived with two brown paper bags. "Hey, lunch time." When I finished my sandwich, I took my paper bag, blew it up and exploded it against the wall. A mistake!

A large mistake. Down the stairs, on the double, came our jailer with a drawn pistol. I'll admit it scared the hell out of me. I decided to behave like a gentleman.

Fifteen minutes later, Lisa relented and paid the fine and an unarmed jailer came down and unlocked the cell. We were free.

Twenty-four years after the paper bag episode, Hugo and I met in the Cotillion Room of the Hotel Pierre, where I was performing in a condensed version of *Music in the Air.* He was now musical conductor for the

New York City Ballet and I was a TV soap opera star, moonlighting in the Cotillion Room. Not bad for two former cell mates who had a memorable lunch in a Connecticut jail.

Our *Pinocchio* opening was quite successful. The children seemed to love it. It had good costumes, plenty of action, and pretty music. We were now into the second week of our tour when we discovered that a piece of scenery was missing. Oh, no! We must have left it at our last performance. We had to do that show minus one piece of scenery. There was only one thing to do: backtrack and pick up the forgotten scenery. The decision was that Lisa and I would take the Packard and retrieve the lost scenery.

Soon after we left, it started to snow, soft, goose-feather snow that floated down and sat on branches to create a winter wonderland. It was beautiful. When we reached the school, I went in to pick up the forgotten scenery. The teacher who handed it to me was very complimentary about our production of *Pinocchio*. I thanked her and inquired about a nice place to eat. She recommended the Hotel Stratford, just a couple of blocks away.

This was the first time Lisa and I had ever been alone, away from work, away from co-workers. She was charming, so was I, so was the Stratford Hotel, complete with fireplace aglow. When a delightful dinner with wine ended, Lisa let down the drawbridge.

"Do you think it would be safe to drive back tonight, Terry?"

I said, "No, there are a lot of dangerous curves on that road, and by morning they will have it all plowed."

Time now for the big question…

"May we share a room, Lisa? You know how I feel about you; you must. I haven't taken my eyes off you since we met."

Pause, a smile. She couldn't possibly have known the excitement that was churning inside me. At long last, to kiss the beautiful ballerina, to touch the untouchable Russian princess. She had seemed so unattainable. Now she was mine, to have and to hold. Whenever I hear the song, "There's a Small Hotel," I remember Lisa and our first night.

8

A Theatrical Tour—What a Trip!

OUR OVERALL TOUR was about three months long. We performed the ballet *Pinocchio* in New England and an evening of dance through the South and Midwest.

A theatrical tour sounds like an exciting adventure, and sometimes it is, but it can be a test of human endurance! Picture ten people in two cars plus a trailer on a journey that never ends. It is the epitome of togetherness.

I spent my days driving down strange roads, haunted by a recurring question, "But am I sure this is the right road?" Then there were temperamental carburetors to be dealt with, plus temperamental performers and bad weather.

We left Buffalo on a highway of glazed ice. By some miracle we managed to keep our vehicles on the road. Many cars and trucks were not so fortunate. We made it to Pittsburgh only to find that city preparing for a flood. Pumps were pumping water out of basements. The Allegheny and Monongahela Rivers meet right in the middle of Pittsburgh to form the Ohio River. All of these rivers were full to overflowing, and the forecast said "rain." So we had a quick cup of coffee and headed south, fleeing before the flood. However, about fifty miles south of Pittsburgh, we encountered a strange sight. The highway simply disappeared in a lake. A small river had gone on a rampage and filled the lowlands with muddy water. Now what should we do? We were truly trapped between the devil and the deep blue sea, with no time to spare. While we were feverishly debating our next move, a car came through from the opposite direction. We decided if that car could make it, so could we. We cautiously inched our cars into the lake. It felt very strange and very dangerous, but there were barbed-wire fences on either side of the inundated road to guide us, so we made it through. How beautiful the highway looked as it emerged from the flood waters, and how grateful we felt to be on a solid piece of cement again!

We performed in theaters and colleges as far south as Vicksburg, Mississippi, and as far west as Nacogdoches, Texas; then we headed north. One gray, wintry morning we were preparing to leave Wichita, Kansas. The company stood around silently as Tony and I loaded the trailer. Everyone was tired and edgy. Lindsey chose this propitious moment to ask Lisa for a cash advance. Lisa said "No," and an argument erupted.

It ended when Lindsey angrily shouted, "You know something, Lisa? You're a bitch!"

I dropped a suitcase, grabbed him by his tie with my left hand, and cocked my right fist to let him have it. I felt him go limp, saw a look of fright in his eyes, hesitated, then asked "Shall I hit him?"

Lisa said, "Yes!" So I let him have it, not all of it, but he went down. It was one of those awful, awkward moments that you wish you could erase, but you can't. We silently got into the cars and headed for Columbia, Missouri.

My parents and my younger sister Kathleen came to see our show in Columbia. I think my dad's hopes for his son sank to a new low when he saw me performing as a male dancer. To his credit, he complimented my performance as the Sorcerer in "The Sorcerer's Apprentice." My mother was delighted with "Tales of the Vienna Woods." It was a charming number. Kathleen's favorite was "Afternoon of a Fawn" by Debussy. The music is so hauntingly beautiful. In this number Lisa displayed her skill as a ballerina and achieved a kind of lovely innocence in the character she created. I thought the varied dances Strawbridge and Parnova presented made for a delightful evening in the theater.

From Columbia, we headed back east where we had a couple of *Pinocchio* bookings left to play.

There weren't a lot of laughs on this tour, but I do remember one: when a high school girl introduced Edwin Strawbridge as "Mr. Edwin, the belly dancer."

It was May and the end of our tour was in sight. Tomorrow would be our final performance of *Pinocchio* in Providence, Rhode Island. One last chance to see Lisa as the Blue Fairy, with her long, blue, cellophane hair and her magic wand. One final time for Doctor Owl to flex his eyebrows and proclaim, "It is my opinion that the marionette is quite dead; but if, through some awkwardness, he should not be dead, then it is a sure sign that he is alive."

Terry and Lisa, 1936

I was pushing the old Packard down a wet highway at dusk some-where in Massachusetts when a car coming from the opposite direction did a left turn in front of me as it headed into a restaurant. I hit the brakes as hard as I could on a wet highway and turned as much as I dared, but I clipped the back end of the oncoming car. The damage to the other car was minimal, but yes, there was a dent.

The car I hit contained a family of four. When the police arrived, which was almost immediately, the children were crying. The Packard with the New York plates was obviously at fault, so off we went to acquaint ourselves with another police station. Strange that our tour should be bracketed by visits to police stations, fore and aft.

Once again there was talk of posting a bond. Once again Lisa dis-played her debating skills. Once again I was the pawn. Finally I got involved in the argument. A mistake. Lisa did a *tour je tête* and exited out the door. Guess what happened to me? You do remember the beginning of this tour, that delightful lunch Hugo and I had in a jail in Connecticut? This was déjà vu time, except that I was alone. One of the officers invited me to join him. We descended a flight of stairs. He showed me to my cell and went back upstairs, and there I sat. This time I was in Massachusetts, but the decor was the same. I often wondered what Oscar Wilde meant when he wrote, "Stone walls do not a prison make, nor iron bars a cell." In my little world, they make a jail. A very effective device to keep you from being where you'd rather be.

As I sat in my sterile cell, I thought that Lisa's dramatic exit was a ploy. She'd be back any minute. After all, the show must go on. The per-formance was scheduled for ten the next morning. Who, pray tell, would play Gepetto the Woodcarver? There was no understudy. She would have to come back and bail me out. But as the sands of the hourglass kept falling, the temperature of my temper kept rising. Where is she, God damn it, where is she? How could she do this to me? Now I was pacing back and forth like a lion in his cage.

Eventually I fell asleep. About 4:00 A.M. the police officer on duty came down to my cell, flanked by Hugo and Lindsey. He was most apologetic, but he said nothing could be done about releasing me until morning. So Lindsey and Hugo tendered their condolences and headed back to Providence. Lisa and I had argued before; she was older and wiser than I. But there was no wisdom in this strategy. She was jeopardizing both the show and our relationship.

Mr. Olmstead, our costume and set designer, played my part. He was the right age for the role. So I learned that I was not as irreplaceable as I had imagined. Worse, I learned that Lisa really didn't care that much. I could never have driven off and left her in a jail.

The man whose car I hit discussed the accident with his insurance agent. When the agent heard the circumstances, a left-hand turn into a drive-in, against oncoming traffic, he advised his client to drop the charges. So I was released from my cell, a free man. A free, angry man, waiting to be picked up by my former lady love. How could she do this to me?

During my wait, I asked a policeman why they held me over- night, and he explained that when an out-of-state car is involved in an accident or moving violation, they require that a bond be posted. No bond was posted for me, so there was no choice.

About two in the afternoon, my rescuers arrived. I was still angry. I maintained a stony silence on the trip to New York City. I'm sure my co-workers and Lisa thought that I would get over my black mood. Maybe in time I would have, I don't know. But when I got to my little room in the big city, I found a letter from my mother. She said that Ralph Moody of the Hazel McOwen Players would like to talk to me about joining his show for the summer. I called him first thing next morning and accepted his offer.

That made me feel ever so much better. In fact I felt so good, I was able to call Lisa and invite her out to dinner. Now I felt secure. No matter how charming the Blue Fairy might be, even if she waved her magic wand, I had made a commitment and there was no turning back.

During dinner, I promised Lisa that I'd see her next fall. But that promise, said with much fervor, turned out to be a slight miscalculation. Thirteen years would come and go before I returned to Manhattan and lovely Lisa. That's show biz.

9

Drumbeats and Heartbeats

*T*HE HAZEL MCOWEN PLAYERS headquartered in Tecumseh, a small town in southeastern Nebraska. Hazel, the oldest of the three McOwen sisters, married an actor named Ralph Moody. They broke away from the family tent show, the Original McOwen Players, and formed their own company, the Hazel McOwen Players. If rivalry existed between the two companies, it was friendly.

Shortly after my arrival in Tecumseh, Ralph asked me if I had ever played drums. I said, "No, but I always wanted to." It was from this humble beginning that I became "the best offbeat drummer in the business." Ralph Moody himself said so. Brad Alexander, actor/trumpet player, gave me lessons on the drums, and I loved it. Tent show performers were supposed to be able to act, do a specialty number, and play a musical instrument. I was getting there: actor, pitchman, drummer.

An evening in the big tent theater kicked off with an overture. Five actor/musicians down right of the stage would play a couple of jazzy numbers like "Twelfth Street Rag" or "Stompin' at the Savoy." One of our musical specialties was tuned pop bottles, which we played to the melody of "The Merry-Go-Round Broke Down." Brad would put water in a pop bottle, just the right amount so it became the note "do" when you blew down on the bottle, pressed against your chin—like kids do. Each musician had one or two bottles tuned to a specific note. When your note was due to be played, you would pop up out of your chair and blow your bottle. This specialty number sometimes ended in a breakup. If a bottle blower was a tad late in standing, or blew a sour note, laughter would follow. Much laughter—sometimes from the other bottle blowers as well.

It was opening night in O'Neill, Nebraska. I was on stage, performing my specialty, selling those boxes of delicious taffy candy, giving out those fabulous prizes, when I spotted a beautiful face in the audience. I found it very hard not to stare. At the first opportunity, I took Bob Evans of the canvas crew up to a peephole in the proscenium where we could look out at the audience, and I showed him the beautiful face.

I said to him, "Between the acts, tell Miss America I'd like to meet her, and to please wait for me."

Later, a smiling Bob said, "You owe me one; she said she'd wait."

When the curtain came down on act 3, I sped through makeup removal and change of wardrobe. Brad turned to me and said, "You act like a man who has a very important date."

"I think I have," I said, and exited. I rushed to the front of the tent and there, by the entrance, stood two young ladies. Miss America introduced herself. Her name was Mary Bowden and her friend turned out to be her cousin, Janice. We strolled into town. Conversation flowed easily. The girls had many questions about our tent show. We stopped at O'Neill's finest restaurant—the only one that was open, really. Here I had an opportunity to look more closely at Mary's face. She was beautiful: dark, wavy hair, white skin, a flawless jaw line, blue eyes, about five-foot-four. She lived in Omaha with her mother and was visiting her grandparents here in O'Neill. I walked the girls home. First we said good night to Janice. I invited Mary to come see our show tomorrow night when we would be doing *Trail of the Lonesome Pine*.

"Will you come alone?"

"Yes."

"Promise?"

"Promise."

Kiss. Delicious kiss.

Mary was eighteen; I was twenty-two. There was a strong mutual attraction between us. It was as though we had been waiting for each other to come along. We spent as much time together as we possibly could the next few days, because we knew that on Sunday morning, the tent would be gone and the actors would have to follow it to the next town. Mary and I had fallen in love, so in addition to acting, selling candy, and playing drums, I had a romance to pursue, and pursue it I did as best as I could with our gypsy schedule of moving to a new town each week.

The Hazel McOwen Players were big on comedy, but we did offer a whodunit called *The Big Scam*. There was one performance of *Scam* that I shall never forget. It was on Wednesday night, July 3, 1937. I was seated at a table center stage. A detective, played by Ralph Moody, began to search my apartment for some stolen money, and he was getting very close to where it was hidden. I sat there, pumping adrenaline. At the peak of this very tense moment, a firecracker exploded right outside our tent. I jumped straight up in the air, knocked the table over, and turned *The Big Scam* into *The Big Laughathon.* We never did get the audience back to the proper mood for a whodunit, but I don't think anyone felt cheated. They left our tent still laughing.

Summer storms with lightning, thunder, wind, and deluge were an ever-present threat. They could damage or even destroy a big tent. Harry, our boss canvasman, always had a watchful eye out for foul weather and an ear tuned to weather forecasts on the radio. If a storm seemed likely, he would double-stake the tent—one additional stake between each pair of existing stakes—then "grapevine it," which meant running ropes up and down around the entire tent from stake to pole.

If a storm began to shape up during a performance, Ralph would tell us to speed up the lines and get it over with before the storm hit. Rain falling on that big piece of canvas made a booming sound that could drown out the actors. Our tent was rather ancient and a bit leaky. It was not unusual, during a rainstorm, to see some umbrellas opened up in the audience. Luckily, most of our patrons were farmers. They know there's nothing anyone can do about the weather. Thanks to Harry's watchful eye and canvas know-how, we got through the summer without any serious storm damage.

Meantime, Mary and I were commuting back and forth across northeastern Nebraska. She came to see me in Orchard. I hopped a bus and met her in Omaha.

That evening, impelled by love, fatigue and desperation, I said, "Mary, wouldn't it make our lives easier if we got married?"

I was too naive to know that marriage doesn't make lives easier, but at that moment, it seemed to me it would.

Mary said, "Did you just propose to me?"

"It did sound like that, didn't it?"

She said, "Yes!"

"Does that mean yes, I will marry you, or yes, it did sound like that?"

She replied, "Both."

For once, I was wordless, so we kissed long and passionately.

"What do you think your mother will say?"

"I think she'll be happy to have someone else look after me. And anyhow, I'm eighteen."

"What about your grandparents?"

"They like you, Terry."

Pause.

"Sounds like we're engaged. But I don't have a ring to give you. Guess that doesn't matter, does it?"

Later, we decided that our wedding would take place in Neligh, Nebraska. This was a county-fair date, and our big tent theater was set up right in the middle of the race track. One simmery summery afternoon, the bride, the groom, and the bridal party of actors assembled at the big tent theater. We were all ready to leave for the minister's, but at that very moment, a car race started. So we all stood there and watched as the racing cars roared round and round us, their dust gently settling on our wedding garments. When the race was finally over, we all drove to the minister's home, where Mary and I were united in holy wedlock. As we left, Cookie, our comedian, delivered the punch line: "Seems to me you people are off to a roaring good start! Hah! Hah!" And so we were.

Labor Day marked the end of the tent show season, and my thoughts were turning to radio. I had done some radio acting, but I wanted to be an announcer.

People told me I had a good voice for radio. So when the final curtain fell, Mary and I hopped a Greyhound bus for Kansas City.

10

This Is Your Announcer, Terry O'Sullivan

SURE NOW, you've heard of the "luck of the "Irish." Well, I truly think I've got a bit of that in me. A legacy from me darlin' grandfather, Cornelius. Within a month, I had a job as a radio announcer at KCMO, the voice of Kansas City. How did I get the job? I started listening to radio announcers, their style of delivery and what they said. It occurred to me that announcers are really pitchmen in a different setting. Their objective is the same as the tent show candyman: sell, sell, sell. When I auditioned at KCMO, I asked if I might give them my candyman sales pitch. It was that performance that got me my first announcer's job.

However, radio was a whole new world to me. It wasn't just using my beautiful voice to say, "This is KCMO. Now, the latest news." I had to cut that news off the Associated Press machine and assemble it into a newscast. And there were all those foreign names and places to be pronounced, correctly.

Then there was the technical side of radio to be dealt with. An announcer sat between two turntables, or record players, but here, too, there was a hazard, because the turntables each had two speeds, 33⅓ revolutions per minute and 78 revolutions per minute. When you were working under pressure, it was easy to screw up. If you played a 78 record at 33⅓, it sounded like a bullfrog giving a sermon. If you played a 33⅓ transcription at 78, it sounded like a tobacco auctioneer. I was guilty of both errors. My immersion into the world of radio was not a tepid bath; it was a cold shower.

One Sunday evening I was running KCMO single-handed. I was in Studio A with the Ozark Mountain Boys. They had just started a song called "The Hatfields and McCoys." This song told the story of a famous feud. While the song was going on, my attention was drawn to a man standing outside the studio window, motioning for me to come out. I knew I had plenty of time, because "The Hatfields and McCoys" went on and on. So I stepped outside the studio to see what this fellow wanted.

He was a performer, in a state of great agitation because his program had been cancelled. I suggested we go into the announce booth to look at the schedule. This guy was giving me a bad time, as though it were *my* fault that his show had been cancelled. He laid one final question on me, and I blurted out, "Oh, God damn it, I don't know." I was standing by a live microphone, which I had neglected to turn off, so right over the top of "The Hatfields and McCoys" came this loud expletive! And on a Sunday evening!

Retribution was swift. I didn't even get two weeks notice.

However, pursuing a philosophy of onward and upward, I made an audition transcription. My intention was to mail it to a radio station in Salt Lake City. If I got a job there, I'd be halfway to Hollywood.

Meantime, my dad's brother, Neal, stopped off in K.C. on his way home to Oklahoma City. When he heard of my career setback, he said he knew the manager of a beautiful radio station in Oklahoma City, and he would see that my audition got into the hands of Mr. Gayle Grubb. So Uncle Neal delivered my audition to Mr. Grubb, and he hired me.

When I left K.C., Missouri, my dad said "When you get to Oklahoma City, be sure to look up Riley O'Sullivan. He works for a newspaper, *The Daily Oklahoman.*"

So I gave second cousin Riley a call. We arranged to meet at Riley's hangout, the Sooner Bar. He loved those drink-a-little, talk-a-lot sessions in a tavern. He seemed to blossom in this setting. He informed me that radio station WKY was owned by *The Daily Oklahoman,* so we worked for the same company. Riley once said, "Every man has a book in him." A simple statement, but it struck a chord. Those words would disappear for years, but one day they would come swimming back into my consciousness to haunt me. I knew sooner or later, I must write the book that is in me.

In 1938, Oklahoma City was sitting right on top of a vast reservoir of black gold. When you stood in a tall building and looked out toward the edge of the city, you didn't see trees. You saw oil wells. All quietly pumping money out of the earth. Some of that oil money found its way into radio station WKY. It was quite a showplace. They had the latest and best equipment, a twelve-piece orchestra, a Four Manual Kilgen organ. NBC picked up some of our musical shows and sent them out on their network.

The article shown on the following page was published in *The Daily Oklahoman.*

It was here at WKY that I met Don Stolz, who many years later became the owner and director of the Old Log Theater in Excelsior, Minnesota. At that time, Don was a student at Oklahoma City University, studying dramatics. We often used drama students in our radio plays. Don and I wound up co-starring in a dramatic series called "Devil's Roost." Devil's Roost, by the way, was a cave. In describing this show, I keep coming up with the word "weird." Actually, it was a popular program and might have run for a long time, had not the writer/director been caught padding the payroll. His abrupt departure left us without a writer. Our other staff writer, Scott Bishop, said he was too busy to write "Devil's Roost" three times a week, but he would write a final episode, and did he ever! He managed to get everyone into the cave, then a massive explosion occurred, which wiped out cave, cast, plot, and counterplot. Never was a show so completely ended as "Devil's Roost."

WKY ON NBC!

Each Saturday afternoon at 4:30 p. m. (C.S.T.) WKY originates the program "Southwestern Stars" for the entire nation. From coast-to-coast it goes, sending the top talent of the Southwest into homes everywhere. Terry O'Sullivan (below) is master of ceremonies on this outstanding network vehicle which is entirely under the direct supervision of WKY. Today's line-up of entertainment promises to surpass all previous endeavors.

Terry O'Sullivan

Article in Daily Oklahoman

Shortly after the demise of "Devil's Roost," I took over the Special Events Department at WKY. One day I got a phone call from the mayor of Okeene, Oklahoma. He wondered if I'd be interested in covering the Rattlesnake Roundup.

"The Rattlesnake Roundup?" queried I. "What the hell is that?"

Terry O'Sullivan and Don Stolz in the cave behind Devil's Roost

He laughed and said, "The country up here around Okeene seems to offer everything a rattlesnake needs for the good life. For one thing, there are lots of small caves where the snakes can hibernate during the winter. In the early spring, they come out of their caves into the warm sunshine. The trouble is, this is also cattle country around here, so every now and then a cow blunders into a diamondback and gets herself bitten. The bite is usually fatal, so the roundup isn't just for fun. It has a real purpose."

I allowed as how a rattlesnake roundup certainly qualified as a special event.

"By the way," said he, "we catch the snakes and bring them into town alive."

"You do? This I've got to see. I'll be there."

Early one Sunday morning, Jack Lovell, our chief engineer, stopped the mobile unit in front of my house. It was an impressive looking vehicle. Actually, it was a white ambulance with big black letters on either side which read "Radio Station WKY Mobile Unit." The entire vehicle was filled with radio equipment for remote broadcasting. I jumped in beside Jack. I was really looking forward to this assignment. It sounded like a real adventure to me. Jack, on the other hand, admitted that he hated snakes, with or without rattles, and would rather spend this beautiful spring day working in his garden. So we had a smiley and a grumpy in the front seat as we headed northwest, toward Okeene, Oklahoma, and the unknown.

After about an hour's drive, the topography began to change. Shallow canyons with exposed rock strata began to slice up the countryside. Beef cattle were contentedly grazing on the new green grass. It looked like a backdrop for a Western movie. Another fifteen minutes and we pulled into Okeene, a small country town that was throbbing with excitement. The main street had a large banner reading "Welcome to the Rattlesnake Roundup."

The mayor came over to welcome us. He was wearing a Western hat, cowboy boots, and a big smile. I asked him when the roundup would get under way.

"Eleven o'clock."

"Good. Maybe you could lead us to a restaurant. We're kind of hungry. And could you join us? I'd like to hear about this roundup."

En route, we passed a grocery store. In the window they had a big display of canned rattlesnake meat. It never occurred to me that anyone would eat a rattlesnake. On the other hand, I had eaten eels, and they are a snake's first cousin. However, there is a point beyond which I do not wish to go. Eels, all right; canned rattlesnake? I don't even want to think about it.

When we seated ourselves in Alma's Cafe, I said, "Now, Mr. Mayor, tell me about this bring 'em back alive routine. Isn't that dangerous? I always heard that a good rattlesnake is a dead rattlesnake."

"Well, you see, Terry, these snakes actually have value. Their venom is used in medicine to counteract snakebites. Then, as you saw in the grocery store, the meat is canned. I know it's not for everybody, but as they say, different strokes for different folks. The skins are tanned for cowboy boots and belts. The hunters work in pairs. One has a gunny sack, the other a pole with a V on the end to pin the snake down, right behind his head. Then you can pick him up by grabbing him right at the base of his skull. Some prefer a pole rigged with a rawhide thong so you can drop the loop over the snake's head and tighten it. Then your partner holds the bag open, you position the snake over the open bag and release the thong, and in he goes, tail first. We ask that everyone reassemble here in the town square at three o'clock. By the way, do you fellows want to hunt today?"

"Ah, I don't think I do, Mayor. How about you, Jack?"

"This is one time I'd like to get stuck holding the bag."

Then I said, "You see, Mayor, we're here to observe this roundup, then describe it to our listeners in radioland, so we do want to go on the hunt, and, of course, interview some of the hunters. We'd like for you to say a few words when the time comes."

"Be happy to. Why don't I send you out with a couple of experienced wranglers? Let's go find Doug Whittemore and Harry Smith."

At eleven, the mayor mounted a podium in the town square and cautioned the hunters to walk slowly and to be careful at all times, for a rattlesnake's bite can be fatal.

"Be back here no later than three." So saying, he fired a pistol at the cloudless sky and the rattlesnake roundup began.

The hunters scattered out through the rugged terrain. Some got into their cars and drove to their favorite spot. We walked in a straight line, about fifteen feet apart.

We had been hunting for about half an hour when Doug said, "Hold it. I see one. Circle around me and take it real easy."

Then I heard the angry buzz that a diamondback makes when he vibrates those rattles at the end of his tail. I followed the sound, and there he sat in a perfect coil, his split tongue flicking in and out, his rattles a-buzz, daring his enemy to approach. Doug slowly moved closer, placed the loop over the rattler's head, tightened the leather thong, and lifted Mr. Rattlesnake up in the air. He was over three feet long. Harry placed the open bag under the tip of the snake's tail, Doug released the leather thong, and the snake disappeared into the gunny sack. Jack and I gave a cheer.

"Men, Methods, and Machinery." That was the motto of *The Daily Oklahoman*, the newspaper that owned radio station WKY. We had just seen the three Ms at work. Our team bagged three rattlers; then we headed back to town. Some people wouldn't go within a hundred miles of a rattlesnake roundup. Then there are those others, daredevils and thrill seekers, who are magnetically drawn to the dangerous and the bizarre.

The roundup was well organized. The hunters emptied their sacks right in the center of the square. A couple of rattlesnake wranglers with long poles herded the rattlers together. If one tried to slither away, a wrangler would slide a pole under the escapee and flip him back with his comrades. The hunters and the curious formed a wide circle around the snakes, leaving lots of air space. People watched with tense fascination. The mayor announced that a total of sixty-eight snakes had been captured, followed by applause and cowboy yahoos.

Then there was a demonstration of how venom is extracted from a rattler. This was a two-man job. The snake's fangs were inserted into a glass with a cloth top, secured by a rubber band. Then the two sacs at the base of the fangs were massaged and the venom thus extracted used to

"Say hello to our radio audience."
c. 1941

make an antitoxin for snake bites.

Shortly after the venom demonstration, the boss wrangler announced, "Any damn fool who'd like to have his picture taken with a diamondback draped around his neck, step right up."

I stepped right up. I guess I did it for publicity purposes, or maybe because I'm a showoff. Anyhow, I was sure I could qualify as a damn fool. The wrangler, using his pole with a V on the end, pinned an enormous rattlesnake to the earth. The V was placed right behind the snake's head. I took ahold of the snake right behind the V, then picked him up as the wrangler draped that snake around my shoulders. I felt a chill that penetrated to my bones. The photographer said "Smile!" The snake laughed. I was transfixed by the proximity of that envenomed head.

Then the wrangler casually removed the living boa from my shoulders and said, "Shove him away from you smartly and release your hold when you get to the end of your shove." I followed his directions. The snake fell at a safe distance. He then went slithering off to join the writhing herd and I returned to planet earth. Nothing like living dangerously to make the adrenaline flow.

The Rattlesnake Roundup made a good special event. Even now, fifty years later, I can still hear the angry buzz of those vibrating rattles when a coiled diamondback threatens to strike.

It's a sound you don't ever forget. I guarantee it.

I worked at WKY for four and a half years. Two of my daughters were born in Oklahoma City, Colleen and Kathleen. My vacations were always spent in Hollywood looking for a job, and finally my persistence paid off.

11
Hollywood Radio

I GOT AN ANNOUNCER'S JOB at KFWB, the Warner Brothers station in Hollywood. It was located near Gower and Sunset, in the very shadow of NBC, CBS, and Columbia Pictures. At last I was really and truly here, in the heart of Tinselville, where big dreams come true—sometimes. KFWB had no network affiliation, so every program we broadcast originated in our studios. On our staff was a sports announcer named Moon Reagan. He turned out to be the brother of Ronald Reagan, the movie star. That seemed very significant somehow; but, hey! I was in Hollywood where things like that happen every day.

Here at KFWB, I encountered something new in the wonderful world of broadcasting: announcers trying to break each other up. I mean they really tried to make you laugh—right in the middle of whatever you might be saying during a live broadcast. It seemed totally insane to me, because I took my career seriously. Consequently, I was a tough customer to break up. When the usual little tricks didn't work, they became more creative. The announce booth was separated from Studio A by a large plate-glass window. Studio A was left in total darkness except when in use. Once when I was in the middle of a lengthy commercial extolling the virtues of Old Mission Tablets for constipation, I heard a light tap on the Studio A window. I glanced up and there, in the window, framed in blackness, was someone's lily-white bare ass. I was shocked! I couldn't finish the sentence I was in the middle of. Instead I blurted out, "Now back to Stuart Hamblen and the Cowboy Church of the Air," flipped off my mike switch, and burst out laughing. To this day, I don't know whose behind I beheld, but I couldn't help wondering if that was how Moon Reagan got his nickname. Not accusing, mind you; just wondering.

I had gone through my initiation rites and was now accepted into the announcing brotherhood. There are times when one can't help saying, "It's a crazy world we live in, isn't it?"

KFWB was truly a different kind of radio station. I sometimes wondered if the K didn't stand for Kasual. We know the WB stood for Warner Brothers. I never did figure out what the F stood for.

Once when I was hosting a recorded musical program, I played the "Hawaiian War Chant." It was pretty exciting music with beating drums, grunts, and "ooh-hahs." Harry, one of the announcers, became so excited that he opened the mike and added a few grunts and "ooh-hahs" of his own. So help me, we got an angry letter from King Kamehameha, objecting strenuously to the intrusive ad-libs. We were astonished that the king listened to our station. Thank heavens the Warner Brothers never tuned in to their radio station or they'd have fired the lot of us. And good riddance it would have been, too.

Along with announcing, I did some community theater. The highlight of my little theater career was a play called *Blithe Spirit* by Noel Coward. I played Charles, the part Rex Harrison performed in the movie.

One of the producers of Twentieth Century Fox had an outdoor theater on his estate in the San Fernando Valley. It had a shell stage, not unlike the Hollywood Bowl, but on a much smaller scale. He permitted the local community theater to use this stage for their plays. This outdoor staging seemed perfect for *Blithe Spirit*, especially the séance scene. It was always very effective. But one night when Madame Arcati the medium was importuning a ghost to speak to her, a coyote lifted his head and right on cue let out a high, lonely wail from a far-off hill. There wasn't a spine in that audience that didn't tingle. I swear that my spine literally rattled. Madame Arcati had made contact with a spirit. It wasn't the spirit she was seeking, but she achieved a psychic phenomenon that was an unforgettable moment both for the actors and the audience.

My career was moving ahead, but my marriage wasn't. It got into trouble shortly after our arrival in California. Mary hated Hollywood. I, on the other hand, loved it. Here there were no career fences; barriers, yes, but they could be breached. In Hollywood, I could become a network announcer. Or maybe a movie star. The latter was a long shot, but it was within the realm of possibility.

I spent a year at KFWB. Then came the big break. I won an audition for the position of staff announcer on the ABC radio network. At that time, it was called the Blue Network. The next step would be to announce a show that would be heard in Hollywood, New York, and every town, city, and whistle stop in between. A real big-time show that would penetrate the living room of the Duncan household in Kansas City. The words, "This is your announcer, Terry O'Sullivan" would cause Norma Jayne's mother to switch off the radio and realize that she had underestimated her erstwhile son-in-law. Her words, "You married my daughter because you knew she was going to be a star," still rankled in my craw, and spurred me ever onward and upward.

At this point in my career, I was totally dedicated to becoming a network announcer. I watched successful announcers: how they dressed, how they deported themselves. I listened to the manner in which they delivered copy. I observed that they seemed to be very much at ease in the company of young ladies and were quite capable of entertaining same with their gift of gab. I studied with Mildred Vorhees, who coached me in the art of reading commercials. I spent a couple of years with Marie Stoddard, who taught voice placement. I can still hear her saying, "It's here," pointing to her nose, "And it's here," hitting her diaphragm. Marie had just turned seventy. Her dyed red hair was piled loosely atop her head to give her more height. She was small but formidable thanks to her perfect posture. Nor had time taken away her vitality. When she was in her prime, she had a 3¼ octave vocal range, which enabled her to have a successful career in vaudeville.

One day Marie gave me a lecture on the subject of drinking. She spoke of the talented performers she had known who had ruined their careers by becoming alcoholics. She concluded with, "You're Irish, so you'd best watch it, Terry." I did watch it. I found that the best place "to watch it" was in a bar, where one could sit and "watch it" disappear.

Because I was so eager to become a network announcer, my ambition, which had spurred me onward and upward, reversed itself and held me back. When I auditioned for a commercial, I would try too hard or become too nervous. An established network announcer had an advantage over me, because this particular audition wasn't the most important thing in his life; therefore, he was more relaxed when he stood in front of a microphone. It was like that maddening game called golf. If you try too hard, you slice or hook. You must learn to give it your all, but in a relaxed manner.

Concentration with relaxation became my new objective, and one sunny California day I received a phone call: "Well, Terry, you won." I was chosen to be the announcer on "Heidt Time for Hires," a musical show that starred Horace Heidt and his Musical Knights. My first network show. Horace had a wonderful personality. He looked as though he could have been on the varsity football team, and he had an ever-ready smile.

I, on the other hand, did not smile when I read my first Hires Root Beer commercial. It listed all the wonderful roots and herbs that went into the making of Hires, giving it that unique and zesty flavor: words like pip-sissewa and sarsaparilla turned this commercial into a verbal steeple chase, but I prevailed—despite my sweaty palms.

Before our show went on the air, Horace Heidt and I would do an audience warmup. We each had a hand-held mike. He would work the right aisle and I the left. The writer of the show would supply us with a few jokes that we could toss in as we interviewed the audience.

One night we had an especially good show and afterwards I was in the mood to celebrate, so I trotted over to the bar across the street for a drink. The first person I saw as I walked in was a young lady I had interviewed during the audience warmup. She smiled when she saw me, so I joined her at her table. I knew her name was Betty Johnson, that she lived in Salt Lake City, and that she was here on vacation. I could see she was quite excited to be with me.

Betty and I had an easy rapport, and the first drink disappeared so quickly we had to have another. She admitted she was fascinated by Hollywood and was thinking of moving here. I told her I once thought about applying for an announcer's job in Salt Lake City, but picked up a job in Oklahoma City instead. I was curious about the Mormons. She was able to answer my questions because she had grown up in a Mormon family. Time, lubricated by cocktails, flowed quickly by.

Betty glanced at her watch and said, "Terry, I've got an early morning flight to catch. I'm sorry, but I have to say good night.

I drove her to the Roosevelt Hotel, promised to write, and said "Good night." I looked at my watch: 1:15 A.M. It couldn't be that late, but it was. Maybe if I went tippy-toe I could slip into bed without waking Mary. No such luck.

I was greeted with, "Where have you been?"

"A couple of musicians from the show and I went across the street to have a drink. We got to talking and that made us thirsty, so we had another drink, and like that. Somehow I forgot about the time."

"I think you're drunk, Terry."

"Aw, come on, I'm not drunk. I'm sorry I stayed out so late."

No reply. She rolled over and turned her back to me. Now she had another reason to hate Hollywood.

"Heidt Time for Hires" was a popular show. Some time in December, the gentleman who represented Hires Root Beer in Los Angeles, George Taylor, and his wife Ellen gave a dinner party at their home. In attendance were Jack Rourke, the director of "Heidt Time for Hires," his wife Joan, and the O'Sullivans, Terry and Mary. It had been a delightful evening, but as I looked around the room, I thought, "Where's Mary?" I hadn't seen her for some time. She had been rather quiet all evening, but now she was nowhere to be seen. I excused myself and quickly checked the bathrooms and bedrooms, then returned to the living room and, with a false bravado, said, "I seem to have lost something."

"What?" asked our host.

"My wife. Has anyone seen her lately?"

No response. All of a sudden it got a bit scary. We started a house search. Nothing. Then we stepped outside. The night seemed vast, dark, and enormously quiet. I called, "Mary." Silence. Where the hell could she be? We returned to the house. I was getting panicky.

George said, "Maybe we should call the police."

Jack said, "Why don't you call home first?"

This I eagerly did. I couldn't believe it when Mary answered the phone.

"Why did you leave the party without saying anything?"

"I was worried about Molly."

"What's wrong with her? She seemed fine when we left."

"She has a cold."

"How did you get home?"

"I took a cab."

I couldn't believe this had happened. These were the people I worked for. The people I wanted most to impress. It was enormously embarrassing to me. Her leaving in this manner was stupid. There were a hundred things she might have said or done, but to just disappear into the night. How could she do this to me?

I returned to the quiet group sitting in the living room and gave a little improvisation. Actors don't lie; they improvise. I told them our youngest daughter, Molly, had been ill. Mary felt she should stay home, but I had urged her to come to the party. They said they understood. I wished with all my heart that I could have understood, but I didn't understand any part of what Mary had done.

The party was over as far as I was concerned, really over. I excused myself shortly thereafter and headed for home. My brain was boiling. "Why? How could Mary do this to me?" By the time I got home, my exterior was calm, but my interior was on simmer.

I started with, "Now, Mary, tell me what happened tonight."

"I told you, I was worried about Molly."

"Wait a minute, we had our regular baby sitter. I gave her the phone number where we'd be, right? Now tell me what the hell really happened."

"I didn't feel comfortable with those people."

"Didn't feel—oh, for Christ's sake, those are delightful, easy-to-be-with people. If they were a bunch of snobs, I'd be the first to admit it."

The thermostat moved from simmer to boil. "What am I supposed to do, send you to charm school? You're a pretty girl; you're well dressed."

"I don't know what to say to them."

"You don't have to be a clever conversationalist, just listen to what they say and laugh at their jokes. What's wrong with those people? Do you feel more at home with Marge, that wino who lives across the street?"

"Don't talk about Marge. You're doing pretty well yourself with the drinks."

"Oh, come on. I don't know what the hell your problem is, Mary, but you'd damn well better get over it, because I'm going to be a big-time network announcer in this town, with or without you. When you do something like what you did tonight, you're working against me, damn it. Is that what you want to do, keep me from getting ahead?"

"If you left it wouldn't make much difference. I hardly see you anyhow."

12

AWOL

On May 8, 1945, the free world celebrated victory in Europe. What a celebration that was! It became known as V.E. Day. After five years, eight months, and seven days, the carnage in Europe ended—but the war in Asia and the Pacific raged on.

On May 15, 1945, I was inducted into the infantry. What a celebration that was! My friends toasted and cheered, convinced that the war would soon be over now that the fighting Irishman had joined the ranks of the walking infantry.

I was nearly thirty years old and the father of three children. The Army was clearly beginning to scrape the bottom of the manpower barrel.

No, I didn't want to go, but I had no choice. Uncle Sam had pointed his finger at me and said, "I want you!"

As I sat on a train bound for Camp Wolters in Mineral Wells, Texas, I decided to approach military life as an adventure. Warfare has always been one of man's principal occupations. Now I would get to experience it first-hand. My marriage had a low tire and a leaky carburetor, so I figured I wouldn't die of loneliness being separated from my wife. I summed it up by saying, "What the hell, go with it, man. Be a good soldier."

It was a sweaty day when we checked into our barracks at Camp Wolters. This was but a preview of coming attractions. It really gets hot in Texas in the summer. It was a wonderful place to play war games, especially if you wanted to lose a lot of weight. It was like exercising in a sauna: sweat, sweat, sweat.

That first day, our sergeant decided a boxing match would be a fun way to start basic training. I volunteered to put on the gloves. My opponent was a worthy one. The first round was a tie, but midway into the second round he landed a haymaker smash into my nose. I truly did see double. I took a swing at the wrong image and lost that fight.

"Okay, Terry, remember the old adage: 'never volunteer in the Army.' Let that be a lesson to you."

Next day during a ten-minute break, Sergeant Siess asked if anyone knew any good jokes. Once again my hand shot up. After all, joke telling was my forté. As I walked up front, I decided to give them "Muldoon, the Strongest Man in Ireland." It went like this:

Ringling Brothers Circus had just received some bad news. Their famous strong man had to have his appendix removed. Mr. Ringling was wondering where he could find a replacement, because it was the middle of the circus season. As he walked by a tent, he saw a member of the canvas crew driving a stake into the ground. The man was swinging the sledgehammer with one hand and the stake was going down into the ground with each blow. He went up to the man and said, "What's your name?"

"My name is Ollie O'Toole, Mr. Ringling."

"O'Toole, I'm looking for a strong man. If you can drive a tent stake with a sledgehammer using just one hand, I think you're our man."

"Thank you, Mr. Ringling. I'd be happy to be your strong man. But when this season is over, you should take a trip to Ireland and look up Muldoon. He's the strongest man in all of Ireland. He can perform unheard-of feats of strength."

When the circus season ended, Mr. Ringling caught a plane for Limerick, Ireland. Then he rented a car and headed for Muldoon's farm. As he was driving down a country lane, he saw a man plowing a field—but there were no horses hitched to the plow. The man was pushing the plow through the earth with his own hands.

Mr. Ringling jumped out of his car, rushed up to the plowman, and said, "Good morning, Mr. Muldoon."

"Good morning, sir...but I'm not Muldoon. My name is O'Gara. Muldoon is the strongest man in Ireland."

"Yes, so I've heard, but here you are pushing this plow through the field with no help. That requires super strength. Tell me, what is it that Muldoon can do that you can't?"

"Why, sir, have you never heard what Muldoon can do?"

"No, I never have, but I'd certainly like to."

"Muldoon can take his little finger, stick it up his ass, and hold himself out at arm's length."

That brought down the house, or would have, had there been a house.

Soldiering was easy for me. I started hunting when I was ten years old, so guns were like old friends. I led an active life, so I could keep up with the eighteen-year-olds on the obstacle course. After a week of basic training, Sergeant Siess appointed me guidon for our platoon.

There was an enormous amount to learn in thirteen weeks: hand grenades, machine guns, how to deal with poison gas, how to wiggle under a barbed-wire barrier, how to keep from drowning, how to, how to, on and on.

The Army had a term for the inept. They were called "fuck-ups." It was rather frightening how consistently the fuck-ups fucked up. I remember we were getting a lesson on the disassembly of the Browning automatic rifle. The Sergeant cautioned, "Be very careful with this spring or it will fly out." One of our inepts was working near me, and when he got to that spring, boing, out it went into the air. As though he had been *trained* to do it the wrong way.

The thing I hated most about the Army was the poverty of it. And the lack of social contacts. After basic training, we were permitted to go to Fort Worth some weekends, but there were approximately five servicemen for every available girl. Those are tough odds. I remember one Saturday night I picked up a girl at a U.S.O. dance. Her name was Alice. She was kind of cute and pleasant, but countrified. When I'd start any boy-girl talk, she'd say, "Aw, fiddle," and giggle. I knew my chances of scoring were mighty slim, but it felt good just to be in the company of a girl. As I walked her home, we cut across a schoolyard. There was a large window in the schoolhouse with a chain-link fence over it to protect it from baseballs.

I said, "Let's go look in that window.

She replied, "Okay."

When she looked in the window, I got behind her. Then I locked my hands into the chain-link fence and Miss Fiddle was my captive.

I said, "Turn around, Alice. Now, kiss me."

She did. Then she realized she was trapped and started to struggle.

Perfect. It only took a few minutes of struggles and "Please, please let me go" to bring me to an orgasm. Miss Fiddle didn't get hurt and I got some much needed therapy. In the Army you learn there's more than one way to play a fiddle.

One day Lieutenant Holt asked me if I would be interested in Officers' Training. I replied, "Definitely."

"Good," said he, and left it at that. I would make more money as an officer and have a better social life.

On September 2, 1945, the Allies and Japan signed a surrender agreement and the world celebrated V.J. Day. The atomic bomb saved the lives of about one million Allied soldiers. The war was finally over. Now all I could think about was getting back to Hollywood and my career. Lieutenant Holt asked me if I was still interested in Officers' Training. I replied, "No, sir, the war is over and I can't wait to get back to Hollywood."

"If you change your mind, let me know."

"Yes, sir, and thank you, sir."

Now I became part of a work crew. We cleaned up buildings and performed menial labor. One rainy day the sergeant in charge asked, "Do any of you soldiers type?" Without thinking, I held up my hand. My motivation was to get in out of the rain. I got out of the rain big time. I got into a permanent assignment in the recruiting office. I had volunteered once too often.

Each morning I would dress neatly, have breakfast, and go off to work in an office, typing re-enlistment papers for eighteen- and nineteen-year olds mostly. It was boring.

I wrote my wife and asked her to write me a letter saying she was ill and wanted me to come home. She wrote such a letter. I took it to the officer of the day, but he refused to grant me an emergency leave.

Now my thoughts turned to the consequences of absence without leave, AWOL. I had a perfect record. I had established an excuse with my wife's letter. The war was over. What could they do to me? Fine me, put me in jail for a short time? Do it! What the hell.

One morning, after breakfast, I caught a bus that took me out to the highway. I stuck out my thumb and the journey began. Catching a ride for a soldier was a cinch in those days.

It felt wonderful to be out of the Army. It felt heavenly to be home again, to see my cute daughters, to see my pretty wife. Mary phoned my parents and told them I was AWOL. My dad called back. He was really upset. According to him, I'd be lucky if I didn't face a firing squad. The game was over, so I turned myself in. My original plan was to hitch a ride back to Texas.

Los Angeles had a large military prison that was run just like Sing Sing. We were permitted to have two cigarettes a day—just enough to keep the habit alive. Lucky me. I was chosen to work on the grease rack— Army lingo for garbage cans. The soldier who told me what to do with the garbage cans carried a sawed-off shotgun, always at the ready, just in case I should try to escape. I spent six days in this prison, and it seemed like a year. When I read that an eighteen-year-old has been sentenced to life in prison, my heart bleeds for him. Life offers so many exciting adventures and wonderful experiences. To miss all that by living in a cage is a horrible tragedy.

On the seventh day I was told to report to the commandant of the

"Then, a soldier...seeking the bubble reputation even in the cannon's mouth."
—As You Like It, *ii.7*

prison. I and eight other prisoners were to be shipped back to our companies. The commandant reminded me of Charles Laughton when he played Captain Bligh in *Mutiny on the Bounty*.

I can still hear him threaten, "If any of you soldiers fuck up in any way on the trip back to your company, you will be returned to this prison and I personally will see that you regret it."

There was a pregnant pause as he looked at each of us with contempt. Then he shouted, "Tenshion!" We snapped up, and he strode out of the room.

I said to myself, "I am going to behave like Little Lord Fauntleroy on that train trip back to Camp Wolters."

The train was loaded with soldiers and sailors returning home from the Pacific Theater. I bought a paperback book, thinking that would keep me out of trouble.

Just before we got to Gallup, New Mexico, an MP announced, "There will be a twenty-minute stop in Gallup. Do not bring any whiskey aboard this train."

Twenty minutes later, we left Gallup. The engineer had to put his locomotive into compound low, so much whiskey had been brought aboard. Every sailor had a bottle taped to each leg, covered by his bell-bottom trousers. Innocent-looking paper bags were all full of booze.

After a bit the train trip became like a New Year's party, with animated conversation and laughter. We went around a sharp curve and a couple of suitcases fell into the aisle. I was sitting in the first seat so I got up to replace them. As I was placing the second suitcase on the pile, a young lady appeared.

She smiled and said, "That's my suitcase. Thank you for picking it up. I want to see if anything got broken."

She opened the suitcase, and what to my wondering eyes should appear but beautiful pint bottles of whiskey, insulated with clothing.

Wide-eyed, I said, "How come?"

As she closed the lid she said, "I'm going to visit my boyfriend in Oklahoma and that's a dry state."

I said, "Well, you were lucky nothing broke. If it falls again, I'll try to catch it. What's your name?"

"Betty."

"Mine's Terry."

She walked back to her seat and my eyes followed her. She was sitting next to a soldier. I could see there was nothing going on between them. In my mind's eye I saw those pint bottles. I didn't want to get into her pants; I wanted to get into her suitcase. "Why don't I try?" I thought. "I know her name; she knows mine. Maybe the soldier will trade seats with me."

So I walked up smilingly and said, "Hi, Betty."

She replied, "Hi, Terry."

Then I said, "Soldier, would you mind trading places with me? I'd sure appreciate it. I'm sitting right up there."

He said, "Sure. No problem."

Wonderful. I could almost taste that Yellowstone Bourbon, so I started.

"I was once an announcer at radio station WKY in Oklahoma City."

The conversation flowed easily. Finally I popped the question: "Betty, could we sample a bottle of that whiskey just to be sure it's not spoiled?"

"Oh, sure," smiled Betty.

So we joined the revelers and shortened the trip to Oklahoma by drinking, talking, and laughing. She left the train in Oklahoma City and I fell fast asleep.

I made it safely back to Camp Wolters. I spent a couple of days in the brig, then had my court martial hearing. I was fined, advised to mend my ways, and released.

I made up my mind that I would just have to be a little patient and soon I would be a free man. I went to the library and checked out *War and Peace*. It seemed in keeping with the times. That must be the longest book ever written. By the time I finished reading all of those pages, I was released from the walking infantry. Hooray!

Winning the Second World War was cause for an all-out celebration. Our country had won in the biggest Super Bowl of all—warfare.

This positive outlook was pervasive. I felt absolutely confident that I would be back in the business in a relatively short period of time—and I was. I won an audition to do the Wheaties commercials on "The Sam Hays News Show," Pacific Coast Network, six mornings a week.

Everything was going great—except for my marriage. We couldn't seem to put Humpty Dumpty together again. God knows we tried, but it just wasn't the way it once was.

One evening, Mary and I were relaxing at a bar across the street from NBC, a popular oasis where radio folk gathered to quench their thirst and have a few laughs. We were sitting at a table with Hal Gibney and his girl. Hal was an NBC staff announcer. The evening had gone rather well until the booze began to take effect, when Mary and I got into a little argument that she settled by throwing a drink in my face. I can't tell you how livid this made me. A slap in the face or a cold drink in the face really makes the adrenaline flow like a faucet. I wanted to come up swinging. How could she do this to me, and right in front of the people I work with? I strode out of that night club dripping and cursing and foaming at the mouth. Next day I was still seething, so I packed my clothes and moved out.

13

Brief Encounter

I MARCHED RESOLUTELY out of my home like a soldier going off to war with flags unfurled and the band setting a smart tempo, but the glamour quickly fades when the parade ends and the business of soldiering begins. So it was with me. I was lonely and not at all sure that I had made the right move when I left home.

One night I drifted into Brittingham's bar, next door to CBS. I was doing some heavy meditating in the "to be or not to be" genre when an attractive young lady walked in and seated herself at a table nearby. I kept trying to meditate and focus on my bourbon, but my eyes didn't want to do that. They kept pulling to the right as though responding to a magnet.

So I said to the bartender, "Vince, ask the charming lady if I might buy her a drink."

When the lady accepted, I moved in beside her and the get-acquainted ritual began. She worked at Columbia Pictures, not as an actress, but as a secretary. However, as anyone could plainly see, she should have been an actress. She certainly had the looks for it. Gina told me she had just gotten off work, that crazy hours were part of the picture business.

We were more like two old friends than two just-mets. We had show biz in common and that made conversation easy.

After several rounds, I said, "Hey, let's go somewhere. I need to move."

So we headed up Gower Gulch, then cut over to Beachwood Drive, a wide boulevard that carried us closer to the Hollywood sign that hangs on the side of a hill.

Gina said, "Where are we going?"

"To the hills," said I.

Then she did a real fast mood change, as though I had pushed her panic button.

She said, "No, I won't go up there. Take me back, please."

"Hey, Gina, relax. I'm no rapist. We're neighbors. We work right across the street from each other, remember?"

But she persisted. "If you don't turn the car around, I'll jump. I mean it."

And so saying, she grabbed the door handle. Then I did a fast mood change. I flashed anger and said, "Oh, for Christ's sake," and executed a U turn that threw Gina's weight against the car door. Her hand on the door handle pushed down, the door popped open, and out she flew. All in a flash.

"Oh, my God! What have I done?"

No sound. I carefully backed the car up to protect her, in case someone came barreling down Beachwood Drive. I was afraid to look. Cement is a tough place for a landing. Then she got up and slowly got back into the car.

"Oh, Gina, I'm sorry. Are you hurt?"

She said, "Turn on the light."

I said, "Sure, but first let me get this car out of the middle of the street."

Then, all of a sudden, she started to weep. "Pent up aching rivers" came gushing out. I was going through all sorts of emotions. As yet, I didn't know where she hurt or how much or anything. Finally the summer storm passed and she calmed down to an occasional sob.

"Gina, are you hurt?"

"I don't think so. My knees are skinned; my hose are ruined."

Then I said, "I can't tell you how sorry I am. Where do you live? I'll take you home."

The trip home was strangely silent. We, who had been such easy talkers, reverted to our status of strangers. It had been a frightening experience for both of us and we wanted to forget it. I never saw Gina again. We were two ships that touched in the night. The encounter didn't sink us, but it did damage our hulls a bit.

This near tragedy had a sobering effect on me. It could have had a much different ending. I could see the headlines: "Girl jumps out of speeding car on Beachwood Drive. She is in stable condition at Mount Sinai Hospital. Terry O'Sullivan, network announcer, is being held for questioning."

A few months before this Beachwood Drive incident, a well known announcer had engaged in a drunken fight with his wife in the front yard of their home. The police were summoned and the fracas got into the newspaper—prominently. He lost a nice announcing job because of it.

Sponsors don't want people of questionable character to deliver their message to the public. As a precaution, there's a morals clause in most contracts so the sponsor can get rid of a performer who gets into trouble. Listen to what Marie Stoddard says, Terry, and remember all those talented people who drank their way out of show business.

Be careful. You've worked too hard to get to this point. Don't throw it all away.

14
Amber Eyes

S CHWAB'S DRUG STORE at the corner of Crescent Heights and Sunset Boulevard was an actor's hangout. It was here, at Schwab's soda fountain, that a talent agent discovered Lana Turner, demurely sipping a soda—dressed in a skin-tight sweater. Almost overnight, she became a movie star, fulfilling and fostering the Hollywood fantasy—to wit: "I could be a movie star, I can act. It's easy. All I need is a chance."

It was here at Schwab's on a sunny California afternoon that I met "amber eyes." It was one of those things that happen on and off the movie screen. Two pairs of eyes meet and lock in on each other like radar. On the screen, appropriate music would be scored to intensify this romantic moment. Off the screen—who needs music?

I broke the radar lock with a question, "Don't I know you?"

The eyes smiled, "I don't think so. I just recently moved here from San Francisco."

The eyes were beautiful, light brown, amber in the bright California sunlight. The eyes had a name, Rene; a slender figure, about five-foot-six, ash blond hair, late twenties. At this moment in our lives, we were both adrift and afloat, so "amber eyes" and "the voice" began to drift and float together.

This was a strange period in my life. I swept out of my home on the crest of a rage. Then after the rage subsided, I wanted to return, but it was like trying to put Humpty Dumpty together again. Mary couldn't forgive me for walking out on her. I countered that it was justified by her behavior; she was not helping me in my career struggle. In fact, she was hindering me. We needed a referee to intercede, but unfortunately we did not have one. I couldn't go home, but on the other hand I didn't want to make a permanent real estate commitment, so I lived in places like motels, small hotels, and garage apartments, moving frequently. As Rene once observed, "If you ever become famous, Terry, every motel on Sunset Boulevard can hang out a sign, 'O'Sullivan Slept Here'."

On Rene's twenty-ninth birthday, I promised her a surprise, something different. We dined at the Malibu Pier, then drove down the coast highway a short distance, to Las Tunas Isle, a small hotel situated remarkably close to the ocean. Each room had a unique motif. The Leopard Room, for instance, had an abundance of faux leopard skin in its decor and a plethora of strategically placed mirrors. My favorite was the Jungle Room, spacious with bamboo walls, fishnet attached to the ceiling by star fish, a king-size bed covered with a burgundy bedspread, picture windows that looked out on the restless ocean, a bar with an artificial palm tree slanted at a rakish angle from which hung a friendly looking ersatz monkey. Rattan furniture, subdued lighting, and the ever-present booming, swishing sound of the surf made the Jungle Room a tropical paradise where, without even thinking, you would start shedding your clothes as you entered. Such was the primitive spell of the Jungle Room.

When morning came, I opened my eyes and saw the fishnet ceiling. I listened to the surf, softer now, not so booming as in the night. Then I looked to my right, but the amber eyes were hiding behind drawn shades. One thing that fascinated me about Rene was that she kept her eyes open when we made love. So did I. This was an additional contact in the ritual of togetherness. As I lay there, gazing at a starfish, I conjured up a South Sea Island fantasy. Wouldn't it be heaven to live on a lush green island, surrounded by sparking blue water? Yes, yes, it would, but what career would I pursue in this island paradise? My voice, my acting ability, would be of zilch value in such a primitive society. Then a voice, perhaps one of my own, said, "Know when you are well off, Terry. Don't make any waves. Leave that to the ocean."

My reverie was interrupted by a soft voice that said, "Thanks, Terry. That was a wonderful birthday party."

As we drove away from Las Tunas Isle, Rene said, "The outside is quite plain looking. There's nothing to indicate what the inside is like."

I replied, "Can you imagine a road-weary tourist stopping there? Our host tells him the only thing left is the Leopard Room. He shows it with pride, and the tourist asks, 'Why do you have a mirror on the ceiling?' Our smiling host replies, 'So you can see what you look like when you're asleep.'"

On a Sunday morning at a motel, somewhere on Sunset Boulevard, when Rene and I had been going together for about six months, I was lying in bed reading when a small child started to cry. My mind flashed back to my home and my three daughters. The crying went on for a long time and it really got to me. I kept thinking maybe one of my daughters is crying like this right now and I'm not there to comfort her. What am I doing here? Why am I doing this? I've got to go home—if Mary will have me. Acting on impulse, as is my wont, I picked up the phone and called Mary. She did not immediately capitulate but said, "Why don't you come by tomorrow and we'll talk about it?" Done! Now, what about Rene? She'll be here soon. What shall I tell her? Tell her the truth.

Later that afternoon, as we lay on the bed staring up at the ceiling, I told Rene what had happened. When I turned to her, I saw a tear run down her cheek. I had cornered myself now. No matter which way I turned, someone would be hurt.

"I'm sorry, Rene, but it was that child crying that got to me."

Thomas Wolfe said, "You can never go home again," but I did, and it seemed to be working. We tiptoed around old skeletons that hung quietly in the closet. We avoided subjects that might lead to skirmishes.

Our home in Culver City was a charming English farmhouse. There was a large sycamore tree in the side yard and a brick patio with a gold-fish pond. After the places where I'd been "camping out," it seemed like a castle. My three daughters slept upstairs, and each morning, early, we would hear a pair of little feet carefully coming down the stairs. It was Molly, our youngest, coming to join us in bed.

I resumed my Sunday morning chore of making waffles for breakfast. I had really missed my three Irish daughters, Colleen, Kathleen, and Molly.

We got through three weeks of togetherness. Then I got a phone call from Rene. She had missed her period.

"Oh, no! Get a rabbit test."

Why do the fates do this to us? Sometimes it seems to me they write the scripts that we act out on the stage of life, with no rehearsal, no director, and no applause.

The rabbit test confirmed our worst fears. Rene was pregnant. Now what have we done, and more to the point, what do we do next? "Oh, what a tangled web we weave when first we practice to deceive." An abortion? Under the circumstances, it seemed the only solution. So Rene had an abortion. Now she needed my support and help to get through a difficult time. I gave them, and this brought us back together.

I had quite a bit of time because now I was a free-lance announcer, which meant I only worked specific shows. It was not my intention to continue seeing Rene, but at this moment she needed me, so the days went by quietly.

One evening I came home and was greeted by Medea. She hadn't killed the children, but she had gotten them out of the house. The stage was set for the climax. She was in a super rage. Then the storm exploded.

"You cheating son of a bitch!"

"What is it, Mary?"

"You bastard, I'll tell you what it is. I found lipstick on your shorts!" She showed me the evidence. "Now get the hell out of here. I'm filing for divorce."

In my heart of hearts, I had wanted to go home. Instead I found myself back in the Blue Goose Motel, with a bed, a chest of drawers, and a canned heat stove.

Rene and I were back together, but somehow it wasn't the same: the separation, the abortion. Perhaps the change was mostly within me. I had made a decision to end our relationship and had failed. Now I couldn't get back to where we were before I'd made that decision. I had misplaced a key and couldn't seem to find it.

My career had been neglected for the past six months. Now I refocused on it with fervor, and new opportunities were shaping on the horizon.

15

The Hot Lights of Early Television

*T*HE VAST WESTERN PLAINS, the formidable Rocky Mountains, and the hot, prickly desert protected the motion picture industry from a young upstart called television, but in the Eastern states, TV was growing by leaps and bounds. The motion picture moguls began to worry about this potential competitor.

Paramount Pictures had a small TV station called KTLA that they doodled with in dilettante fashion. It was located just outside the Melrose entrance to the big Paramount movie lot, like a doghouse where you keep your pet.

One day a Paramount executive, on returning from a trip to New York, called a meeting and announced to his astonished constituents, "Gentlemen, I believe the time has come to hedge our bets. Let's, at least, stick our big toe into the murky waters of television. I've seen Milton Berle."

So they imported a TV producer from New York, gave him a small bag of gold, and said, "See what you can come up with. We want three hours of programming every night for thirteen weeks."

A director that I'd worked with at NBC, Fred White, was recruited for this bold experiment. When the search for talent started, he told his boss, "Terry O'Sullivan is telegenic." Those words got me an audition, and that audition got me thirteen weeks of chaotic employment in the exciting new world of television as announcer, emcee, host, or whatever.

It was a new medium and there were new problems to be dealt with. Hot lights, for instance. Al Jarvis and his "Make Believe Ballroom" was invited to join our group. He was a disc jockey who used the 78-rpm type records. One of these records was left on the top of a credenza when the show started. When the show was over, that record was warped. The heat from the lights was sufficient to cause the record to bend where it hung over the edge of the credenza. Hot lights? They really were.

This was a great way for me to break into TV because the standards were not too high. We didn't have much rehearsal time, so perfection was not demanded of us. Actually, some of the shows were quite good because they were spontaneous and unrehearsed. Management booked talent with established acts: singing, dancing, and stand-up comedians for variety shows. Interview shows were very popular. I recall one such show where we got into a discussion about the future of television, and I made an outlandish prediction.

I said, "One thing we know for certain, soap opera will never be on television."

The person sitting opposite me asked, "Why?"

"Because," said I, "the actors could never learn all those lines every day."

Did I ever have to eat those words! I spent about fifteen years of my life in TV soaps eating those words. Perhaps it would be more accurate to say learning those words, for that is what I had to do, learn those words—day after day.

We had a few sponsors at KTLA, like Mad Man Muntz, the used car dealer. How far wrong could you go with a commercial for Mad Man Muntz? You'd have to trip and fall to blow that one. On Saturday nights, Beryl Wallace, a headliner from Earl Carroll's night club, and I co-emceed an audience participation show. I can't say we set any new standards for audience participation, but we did get some laughs and the audience applauded.

Television brought us new challenges and new horizons; it also brought us new faces. Laura Greenwood was such a one, a beautiful new face with green eyes and a dimple. One night after the hot lights were turned off, several of the KTLA group went out to the Sunset Strip to have some fun. It was when I danced with Laura that our relationship changed from casual to close. It was 1948, and the music of that time was romantic. We danced to "Moonglow," and we became one with the music. As we walked back to the table, I asked Laura if she liked the beach. This question produced a big smile, and "I love it." So we made a date for a Saturday morning trip to Santa Monica.

Saturday was a perfect day at the beach. We walked barefooted through the sand. Then I took her hand and we ran to the water. Laura looked beautiful in a bathing suit, the epitome of womanhood, combining femininity with strength. She was a strong swimmer, yet she had an aura of softness about her, a fascinating combination, and we shared a love of the ocean.

What is this irresistible magnetism that the ocean exerts on beach lovers? It is a combination of sights, sounds, and sensations. The surf roars as it flings itself against the shore, then hisses angrily as it retreats, vowing to attack again. White gulls laugh as they wing their way down the strand. Pelicans, looking as though they belonged to another age, dive straight down into the ocean like spent arrows in their quest for fish. Sandpipers on delicate, spindly legs retreat in front of an incoming wave, as though fearful of getting their feet wet, then follow that wave back out as they probe for food in the wet sand. The warmth of the sun, tempered by a cool ocean breeze, and the sparkle of the restless ocean is irresistible. Some say our ancestors came from the ocean and a far-off voice calls us back, so we brave the chill and plunge into the blue water.

One day at Santa Monica beach, when the sea was very rough, I dove under a big incoming wave, came up in a water trough, and found myself face to face with a seal. He was surprisingly close. I can still see his wet face, bulging eyes, and spiky mustache. Our eye to eye contact lasted about one second, then we simultaneously dove and sought more hospitable territory. This chance meeting was accomplished with the precision of the Radio City Music Hall Rockettes. We came up out of the sea on the same beat, made eye contact with utter precision, then dove simultaneously. Hours of rehearsal couldn't have improved our flawless timing. However, our mutual eagerness to terminate this chance meeting caused me to question that ocean ancestry theory. The seal and I did not behave like long-lost cousins. It was more like the unexpected meeting of a Martin with a McCoy on a mountain trail in Feudsville, Kentucky.

Our day at the beach was beautiful. We ran, we swam, we sunned, and we talked. Laura asked me about myself. I told her that I was getting a divorce. The day in court had been set. I had three daughters and was doing rather well as a free-lance radio announcer. Then she told me of her aspirations. She wanted to be a movie star, but for now she would love to do extra work. I said, "Maybe I can help you get into the extras union." So the curtain fell on act 1.

16

North to Big Sur

IG SUR, CALIFORNIA. A travel folder described it as "a rugged stretch of coast, mostly undeveloped, located 375 miles north of Los Angeles and about 30 miles south of Monterey, on Coast Highway 1." That sounded like the retreat I was seeking: rugged, undeveloped, on the ocean, large campground. Perfect. It took some persuasion, but Laura finally agreed to join me on this "get back to nature" adventure.

Thirteen weeks of early television's hot lights and improvisational type programming had left me with a perpetual tic, an eyelid that would not stop fluttering. It was hazardous for me to stroll down Sunset Boulevard because women thought I was winking at them.

The journey was one I shall never forget. As we drove north on the coast highway, we watched a fiery red ball set the clouds aflame, then slowly sink into the Pacific. I felt an urge to toast this spectacular sunset, so I opened a bottle of bourbon. As darkness descended, the road began to twist and turn. Then we began to encounter patches of fog and the highway became quite wet. At this point I realized that we were "on vacation." Aided and abetted by sips of bourbon, I began to loosen up and sing. Drunk? No, no, just feeling good. And free. Free of TV. On the return trip, which was accomplished in broad daylight, I saw this stretch of road for what it really was—a spectacular death trap, with hairpin curves and cliffs that dropped hundreds of feet to the rock-strewn ocean below. I had driven this steeplechase at night, in patchy fog, with alcohol for my co-pilot. I felt a delayed adrenaline flush when I looked over a cliff and realized how dangerous the trip up to Big Sur had been. The luck of the Irish?. The Irish need luck, they do so many stupid things.

When we arrived, we discovered there really isn't a town called Big Sur, as I had imagined. The travel folder had described it accurately: a rugged stretch of coast, mostly undeveloped. There's a motel, then a mile further north overlooking the ocean is Big Sur Hot Springs, where you can soak the misery out of your bones. Further on, a restaurant located up above the highway, and finally the Big Sur River campground—our destination. The river looked more like a stream, but perhaps they named it during the rainy season, or perhaps the redwood trees that line its banks throw things out of perspective. Their size makes people feel like midgets, and rivers look like streams. Here we pitched our tent and found that which we were seeking, a retreat, far from "the madding crowd's ignoble strife." And a bonus, we had access to a private beach. Across the highway, then down a gravel road, through a barbed-wire gate, around a curve, and there it was, the beach. In the form of a private cove. Heaven.

One morning we went to our cove at dawn. The gulls were winging by and the tide was moving out, leaving behind much wreckage on the shore. The poet in me responded.

Daybreak

Day hurls a spear that sticks in the side of night;
Red blood of Dawn oozes from the Eastern wound
And spreads across the garment of darkness;
Golden warriors advance from hilltop to Heaven,
And pierce the silver armor of the moon,
Pale as a corpse it lies on the gray sky:
The morning star feels a stab of crimson;
Night retreats and dew of death descends to earth:
The victorious sun rides triumphant through his sky.

The wind retreated with darkness,
The tide followed the moon,
The ocean breathed easily;
But the sand was strewn with wreckage:
Green and amber seaweed,
Shell fortresses—unmanned,
A lobster whose heavy armor failed,
A starfish fallen from his watery sky.
An underwater battle had been fought here,
But it was indecisive
And the forces were regrouping.

We sunned, we swam, we fished—not seriously, but we caught a couple of ocean perch, which we took back to our camp in the redwoods, where we fried them for dinner. Here, on the Big Sur River, we found that which we were seeking: beauty, quiet, and simplicity.

When darkness came, nocturnal creatures would emerge out of the shadows: small bandits, wearing harlequin masks. Woe to the careless camper who left any edibles lying around, for raccoons are formidable foragers. Their front paws are much like a person's hands, which enables them to open most any container with the exception of a tin can, and I think they might solve that if you left a can opener nearby. These masked bandits were quite bold. When we turned our flashlight on them, they would stare right back at us, the light reflecting from their eyes. This was their home. We were the intruders, and we were treated as such.

One night, the clouds sailed off on a journey to the east, and the moon paid us a visit. The night was exquisite, with shadows, and deep mystery. I wanted to remember this night always, so I painted a picture with words.

Tapestry

I will weave this night into a lovely tapestry:
For colors there will be the orange glow of our fire;
The warm red of your kiss; silver of the moon;
Gray swirl of smoke, and ebony of deep shadows;
Then will I weave the ripple of your laughter
Into the music of the waterfall;
Copy designs the tree limbs cast upon the grass;
Sew the cricket's song across the night's silence;
And trace the shadowy path along the stream:
But the central figure will be your voice,
And clustered round it your whispered words of love.

On our last night, we went to Nepenthe, a Greek restaurant strategically located up above the coast highway with an ocean view of far horizons, where distant ships move ever so slowly and sunsets linger. We dined on shish kebab and rice, with baklava for dessert.

I asked our waitress, "What does Nepenthe mean?" and she said, "It's a Greek word which means no sorrow."

We smiled, because sorrow seemed a world away from us that evening. I was falling in love with Laura, and sorrow was that tiny ship disappearing into the dusk. We were that lucky couple who finally found each other and discovered life's meaning in each other's eyes.

Next morning, we quietly folded our tent, said good-bye to Big Sur, and headed south. My eyelid no longer fluttered; my hand was steady on the wheel. Big Sur had worked its magic.

17

But Is the Masked Spooner Telegenic?

*M*AN'S QUEST FOR THE NEW and different is never ending. Sometimes the simple act of mixing two old ingredients together will produce a brand new product. My friend Jack Rourke, an independent producer, tried this simple recipe: he mixed speaking and crooning and created spooning. Instead of crooning the lyrics of a love song, he would spoon them—speak them, really—with a warm, romantic voice, backgrounded by an instrumental arrangement of the song. This he sent out on the Don Lee Mutual Radio network, late in the evening, and before long, young ladies started swooning over his spooning.

He gave the Spooner an aura of mystery by dressing him in a black cape topped off with a black mask and sent him to the Hollywood Brown Derby for lunch, flanked by two athletic bodyguards. Why bodyguards? To protect the Masked Spooner from overzealous fans, who might otherwise tear off his mask in their wild desire to discover the true identity of their hero. Even show-biz oriented Hollywood was agape when the Masked Spooner and his entourage paid a visit to the Brown Derby.

Life Magazine did a picture story on the Masked Spooner. This only intensified the mystery and caused more people to ask, "But who is he?"

These were exciting times. Television had recently emerged from the experimental stage and was finding its way into the mainstream of American life. It was inevitable that the Masked Spooner would gravitate toward TV. He was very visual. What he *did* was not very visual, but in the early days of anything, everything seems possible.

Jack Rourke's eyes were brimming with boyish enthusiasm as he told me about his plan to put the Spooner on TV. He saw it like this: as he spooned the lyrics, Laura and I would act out the words to the song.

I said, "Wait a minute, Jack. You mean we would act out the lyrics on camera? Impossible! Sarah Bernhardt would fall on her ass trying to do that. You'd need emotions that you could shift like gears in a car. All right, take the lyrics of a current song, 'you're breaking my heart 'cause you're leaving, you've fallen for somebody new.' So you can put fake tears on your cheeks, but where do you go from there? Or the lyrics 'I wake up smiling for there's no love like your love.' Sure I can smile lasciviously as I'm lying there in bed, but I'd have to do the Kaiser commercial in my pajamas. You know, Jack, I saw something on TV that might work for us. Dancers were dancing behind a scrim, so you saw them in silhouette. Why wouldn't that work? The Masked Spooner is in black; the moving figures would be in black. It would work beautifully with 'When They Begin the Beguine,' for instance. You could have a couple of palm trees for atmosphere. Laura and I could meet center stage, do a few dance steps, embrace, then she leaves me and I suffer. Sort of dream-like and stylized. And with Laura playing the girl, you wouldn't have any trouble distinguishing girl from boy."

It took a lot of persuasion, but Jack finally agreed to go with the scrim.

The Don Lee Television studios are located on top of Mount Lee. Even if you've never been to Hollywood, you've probably seen the famous Hollywood sign attached to the side of Mount Lee. It appears on television shows and picture postcards. The Don Lee TV studios are located above the sign, right on the top of Mount Lee. These studios had been there through the experimental years of TV and some of the equipment was rather outdated. It was to the Don Lee studios that Jack Rourke took his show, "The Masked Spooner," sponsored by Kaiser Fraser automobiles.

Opening nights are always exciting and nerve wracking, but finally the little red light went on and the show began. The Masked Spooner flanked by his two bodyguards made a dramatic entrance into his den, and with the assistance of his lackeys, seated himself in a high-backed, antique chair behind a table. He started to spoon the words to "Begin the Beguine," but his microphone was dead, so the director cut to me seated in my library looking longingly at a picture of Laura.

Then the dolly man would slowly push the camera into a closeup of Laura's picture, enabling me to get out of the library and into the tropical set. Apparently communication between cameraman and dolly man broke down. The dolly man pushed the camera too far, and the cameraman could no longer focus on Laura's picture. He hissed, "Hold it, for Christ's sake." As I left the library set, I thought to myself, "I'll bet our viewers heard that." They did. I moved quickly to the set framed with palm trees. By this time, the Spooner's mike was working and his romantic words were floating

The Masked Spooner

on the music. Laura and I started toward each other from opposite sides of the set. We moved slowly, romantically toward each other, in extreme profile. Shortly before we came together, we stopped. I placed my hands on Laura's upper arms, but because we were in silhouette, it looked as though I had reached out and filled my eager hands with Laura's more than ample bosom, turning this romantic moment into the laugh of the evening for our TV viewers. I was blissfully unaware of what had happened, and as I moved toward the commercial set, I thought, "Hey, the Beguine number went great."

The beautiful Kaiser automobile, whose virtues I was to extol, was sitting on a turntable. On a word cue, it was supposed to start slowly turning, enabling me to point out its unique features as it rotated in front of me. When it didn't rotate, I had to move around, and this threw my timing off. I stumbled on to the end of the commercial; then the turntable started to move.

The show was a shambles. People who saw it were still laughing the next day. Henry Kaiser said, "I don't think the Masked Spooner is telegenic." The *Hollywood Reporter* said, "The Masked Spooner was the lucky one. He wore a mask."

Jack Rourke said, "You and your silhouettes. Next time keep your hands where they belong."

P.S. There wasn't any next time.

18

"The Jack Smith Show" Goes to New York

*T*HE JACK SMITH SHOW" was a fifteen-minute musical interlude each evening at eight on the CBS Radio network. Jack was an upbeat performer who sang with a smile. Frank DeVol and his orchestra supplied the music, and to put the icing on this musical cake, Jack would invite a top-flight chanteuse to join him in his song fest; singers like Doris Day, Liltin' Martha Tilton, Margaret Whiting, and Dinah Shore.

At this time, Dinah Shore was starting her comeback. She was married to George Montgomery and had taken a hiatus from show biz to have a child. Her agent got her a booking in the Persian Room of the Waldorf Astoria Hotel in New York City. The club date was for the month of January in 1950. The only way Dinah could take advantage of this offer, due to contractual commitments, was to move the entire "Jack Smith Show" back to New York City. It took a bit of doing, but details were worked out and "The Jack Smith Show" headed east. I was invited to tag along since I was the voice that extolled the virtues of Oxydol, the whiter, whiter soap for a whiter, whiter wash. For me it would be a wonderful vacation from an estranged wife who wouldn't give me a divorce and a lady love who thought it was time to get married. That scenario is called a triangle, and it can be quite painful to all parties involved.

That first evening in Manhattan, a group of Jack Smith people got together to go "on the town": Margaret Whiting, Frank DeVol, our writer Glen Wheaton, and me. We started at the Blue Angel and went from there. The sensible people dropped out one by one, but I wasn't ready to go to bed; this was my big homecoming celebration. I had been away from New York for thirteen years. I asked the cab driver if he knew of any clubs that might still be open.

"You bet," said he, and a few minutes later he deposited me on the doorstep of the Savannah Club. I returned to the Shelton Hotel quite late, mission accomplished. "Big homecoming celebration."

My wake-up call came at noon. After hanging up the phone, I stared at it.

"Is it possible?"

I picked up the Manhattan phone directory and turned to the Ps. There it was. Parnova, Lisa.

"Should I? Yes, of course. Just dial!"

Lisa was enormously surprised and genuinely delighted to hear my voice. She had married and now had a seven-year-old son. However, she was a widow, so we made a date for dinner. I was really excited at the prospect of seeing her again. What would the beautiful ballerina be like after all these years?

I was seated at a table in Sardi's Restaurant, chosen so I could see her when she arrived. I felt the pulse quicken when Lisa came into view. Trim as ever, long black hair done up in a bun at the back. Looking remarkable for a lady of fifty. We had much to talk about and we did, on this and other occasions, but the blue fairy had lost her magic wand. Now we were old friends.

"The Jack Smith Show" was a Monday through Friday commitment. It occupied three hours of my day, in the late afternoon and early evening, leaving a goodly amount of time for social activity. There was a phone number in my little black book alongside the name, Jean Williams. A friend had given me her number, so I called.

Jean suggested that we go to a supper club in Greenwich Village, where a small combo provided music for dancing. I liked her choice of supper clubs. I liked her looks and her personality. It had been a long time since I had spent an evening like this, really enjoying myself, with no clouds in the sky and no threats of rain. Jean was a model. She had come to New York to escape a Hollywood romance that had gone awry.

"Shall we dance, Jean? Let's dance forever. Like Fred Astaire and Ginger Rogers, over the clouds and into the sunset."

Jean's gone-awry romance had driven her to a psychiatrist. Not your common everyday variety, but an orgone therapist. This was a new and somewhat bizarre branch of psychiatry. Part of the treatment involved sitting in a box to meditate. Yes, Jean had a box in her apartment in which she sat each day. It seems that the rays a person generates and sends out during these meditations would hit the side of the box and bounce back, like "that which the fountain sends out returns again to the fountain." Or something like that.

Perhaps my social calendar was a bit too full. Also, I had trouble sleeping in midtown Manhattan. It was noisy. The cabbies never stopped honking their horns. After a couple of weeks of New York type living, I caught a cold. Then I woke up on Sunday morning with no voice. I mean zilch. I was like Sampson minus his hair. My voice was my means of livelihood. Where the hell had it gone?

I phoned Jack Smith and whispered, "This is your announcer, Terry O'Sullivan."

"My God," said Jack, "What happened?"

"Someone stole my voice," said I. "Should I call the house detective?"

He gave me the name of a voice specialist who made his living tuning up the vocal chords of actors and singers. I promised to see "the specialist" first thing Monday morning.

The specialist did all sorts of things to my vocal instrument. He sprayed, he fiddled, he fumed.

"See if it works now," said he. I spoke, not well, but I made a human sound. Hooray!

An hour later it was gone. I phoned Jack and said, "We'd better get an understudy." He agreed. So for the next three days, Ken Roberts told our listeners all about that Oxydol sparkle.

Meantime the specialist plied his magic. Finally my voice returned. I stopped drinking. I curtailed my social activities and promised the gods I would behave in a more orderly fashion. Dinah Shore was very sympathetic; singers know what a disaster it is when your vocal chords don't function.

Margaret Whiting had a couple of house seats for the big Broadway hit *South Pacific* and invited me to join her. What a wonderful show that was, with Ezio Pinza and Mary Martin!

The loss of my voice was like a harbinger of evil things to come. A week later, I received a phone call from Sam Hays in California. He said, "I've got some bad news, Terry." Then he proceeded to tell me that General Mills, makers of Wheaties, the Breakfast of Champions, had restructured their advertising budget. Sam and I had been doing ten news shows a week. They were cutting this schedule to five a week, and Sam would do his own commercials. No more would I open the program by asking "Had your Wheaties today?" My mind flashed back to a summer morning when I was reading a Wheaties commercial, enthusiastically, with a smile in my voice, when suddenly I felt as though I was going to faint or pass out.

As soon as the newscast was over, I said to Sam, "What the hell happened to me during that second commercial? I felt like I was going to faint."

He chuckled and said, "Your stand-up mike was swaying. We just had an earthquake."

"Thank God. I can't tell you what a strange feeling that was."

That month in New York had been a wonderful vacation. Now it was time to shoulder my full field pack and march to the beat of a different drummer.

Laura met me at the airport. What a beautiful girl she was. In New York's teeming millions I saw no one that compared with Laura. I gave her a kiss, a bottle of Shalimar, and a poem I had written.

Good night, my luscious woman, what has changed you so?
Your lips on which red kisses abundantly did grow,
Now blossom only yellow yawns, tiresome and slow;
Good night my mad obsession, Good night my wild desire;
Those green and wicked eyes of yours that charmed me with their fire,
Now haze like distant mountain tops when daylight does retire.
Good night, my lovely statue, prize of nature's art,
The gods of sleep have kidnapped you and left an empty heart.
Gracefully they've posed you on a misty lake of white,
A lovely unseen picture in the gallery of night.

I had given up my apartment when I went to New York, so now I was one of Hollywood's homeless. Laura invited me to spend the night with her and her roommate, Virginia. They lived in a small house in Laurel Canyon. I did love this lady. It wasn't an achievement; it was a natural phenomenon like the rising of the moon, seemingly from nowhere, but there it is, dominating the night sky.

Next morning the two dogs were barking. I mean raising hell. I got up to see what was upsetting them. When what to my wondering eyes should appear but my wife, flanked on either side by a private detective. I cannot describe what this did to me. It was more than an invasion of privacy. It was more like an invasion of my soul. I was caught! Trapped! Treed! Name it. There I stood in my p.j.s amid barking dogs and private detectives, and occupying center stage was my wife, who had just trumped my ace. But good! Curtain!

She knew when I was due back in town. She set a trap and I, stupid idiot, walked right into it. When I met Laura, I was in the process of getting a divorce. Mary had started an action and a court date had been entered in the records. When that day arrived, she failed to make an appearance. When questioned about her failure to appear in court, she would only say, "I changed my mind." Further questioning brought more rewarding statements like, "I don't know; I guess I forgot." So the stage was set for one of the old classics, a drama called "Cat and Mouse."

Later that morning I phoned my lawyer and told him about Mary's early morning raid in Laurel Canyon. He confirmed my greatest fear, "Yes, this is a setback for our side in the upcoming trial." But I couldn't turn back now. A day in court was my only hope of bringing the "Yes, I will. No, I won't," syndrome to some kind of a conclusion.

The Laurel Canyon incident was far-reaching. It had a devastating effect on my relationship with Laura. The shock and embarrassment of being flushed out of a love nest—so called—took its toll. Now there was the valid fear that Laura would be subpoenaed and would have to testify in court. There was a possibility that the media would cover the trial. This upcoming divorce case had all the elements that make for good reading in the *Daily News*. To avoid this catastrophe, we sent Laura up to Palm Springs.

Once you get caught in a downdraft, it's astonishing how it tends to continue. I received a phone call from Al Hotchkiss of Dancer, Sample, and Fitzgerald, the ad agency that handled "The Jack Smith Show." Al opened the conversation with a familiar line: "I've got some bad news, Terry." He proceeded to tell me that they were starting a new ad campaign to promote the sale of Oxydol. Instead of calling it the whiter, whiter soap, Oxydol would be touted as a deep cleaner. The new pitch was, "Oxydol is deep cleaning, deep cleaning, deep cleaning," the announcer's voice descending right down to the bottom of the scale as he read the line.

"You've done a great job for us, Terry, but we need someone with a basso profundo to effectively deliver the new message. Sorry."

Wonderful. No income and an expensive trial coming up. How good can it get?

I had to fly my key witness in from Florida. Sylvia used to live down the street from us. Her marriage, too, had gone on the rocks, at which time she and my wife had done some double dating. She agreed to stand up in court and tell all. Why? For an all-expenses- paid trip to L.A. On me, the once prosperous announcer. One more entry into the debit ledger.

The day in court was like a wake. Old friends assembled to observe the death of a marriage, the death of a love affair, and damn near the death of me.

The court action played itself out in this fashion: Mary proved me guilty with the early morning shootout in Laurel Canyon. I proved Mary guilty with my key witness, Sylvia. Had there been an innocent party and a guilty party, the innocent party would have been granted a divorce. But since there was no innocent party, no divorce was awarded. This was 1950 in California, and this judge abided by the then existing statutes. Case dismissed.

My world had collapsed. As I sat in my lonely room, it seemed to me I had two choices. I could go to New York, or I could kill myself. No, there was a third option. I could have a drink. Where? Don the Beachcomber's, with its tropical decor and delicious rum drinks.

As I walked into the Beachcombers, someone said, "Terry!" I turned, and there sat Len and Ann. They invited me to join them. Ann was a girl Friday from Dancer, Fitzgerald, and Sample ad agency, an old friend, so she knew some of my problems. As the rum flowed, Len spoke of his parachuting out of New York under similar circumstances, with a safe landing in Hollywood. He was currently in the appliance business and doing well.

Destiny had spoken. I had been shown the way out of the swamp in which I was floundering.

Next morning, my decision held firm. Move to New York. I would stop off in Kansas City and see my folks, then proceed to the big city. My love affair was dying a slow and agonizing death and there wasn't anything I could do to rescue it. "He who fights and runs away, lives to fight another day." Go! Better than slowly sinking in this swamp. The time has come. Sell your car, buy a plane ticket, and get out! Now!

There was a small farewell party. Laura looked lovely in a white dress that emphasized her beautiful tan. Why didn't God create more Lauras? Too expensive, I suppose. Now I didn't want to leave. But you can't make a toast at your farewell party and say, "Surprise! I've decided to stay."

I kept thinking of my three beautiful daughters: Colleen, Kathleen, and Molly. When would I see them again?

Shortly after the plane took off, I felt rather ill. I went up to the stewardess and said, "Do you have any Dramamine?" I didn't hear her reply. Next thing I knew, I was lying in the aisle and someone was loosening my collar. When I got back to my seat, they gave me an oxygen mask that I wore all the way to Kansas City.

I wrote this poem.

Last Journey

One day to escape you I will journey to the moon,
As I walk happily among its silver craters,
Light and free in its rarefied air,
I will hear your beautiful laughter,

And turn and find you standing there.
You will smile, your wonderful smile,
With bitchery sparkling in your eyes,
And say, "It was more beautiful from the earth,
Wasn't it, darling?"
Then I will run to you, with giant steps,
But you will move ever ahead of me—without moving,
And still smiling you will wave good-bye, again.
I will cry out, "Please, love, leave me something,
Take all of yourself, even your thoughts,
Leave me one autumn leaf to remind me of our summer,
Leave me the hand you wave so casually,
One magic hand with tapered fingers
One lovely flower-like hand to look at
Through the bleak eternity of tomorrow."
But you will disappear into starry space.
Then as I look around I will find craters of cracked lava,
And a cold wind will blow cosmic dust into my eyes.

My parents met me at the airport. My mother said, "You look pale, Terry. Are you all right?"

I said, "Yes, I just need some sleep."

Next morning I awoke and found myself in an emerald world. It was mid-June and Kansas City had been blessed with a rainy spring. After the sun-bleached hills of California, I saw green and felt at home. How sweet it was to be waited on and treated like the Prince of Wales. It had been a long time since such had been my lot.

I spent two wonderful weeks amid the green, green grass of home. My folks thought I should stay longer, but I was restless. I wanted to get started in New York. It had been good to me in the past, so why not now?

I had one awkward problem. I was broke. That day in the divorce court, which accomplished absolutely nothing, had cost me a bundle. There was an O'Sullivan household in Van Nuys, California, with three little girls that needed subsidizing, and a New York apartment yet to be financed. An unemployment check just couldn't keep an ark of that magnitude afloat. So at age thirty-five I had to "screw my courage to the sticking point" and say, "Dad, I wonder if you could help me out? My situation is like this: I'm out of chips, but I'll guarantee you it won't stay that way long."

He sagely observed, "New York is a tough town."

"Not for me, it isn't. As a free lance announcer, I've done most of my work for advertising agencies, like Young & Rubicam; Sullivan Stauffer, Coldwell & Bayles. Their home offices are in New York City, so it's not as though I'm going there cold. I'm already established with most of the big ad agencies. It will take a couple of months, but I'll get it going."

So Timothy Aloysius came through with, "I'm counting on you." It's good to have a good family. Very good.

19

New York City, 1950

NEW YORK CITY IN 1950 was a land of opportunity for performers. Television had come into full bloom. Casting people were actually looking for actors instead of avoiding them. This was the era of Ed Sullivan, the "Robert Montgomery Show," "Your Show of Shows," and "The Honeymooners."

I had come to New York at an opportune time.

Soon after my arrival, I was introduced to the Actor's Lounge, on the third floor of the RCA Building. A place to check your phone service, take the weight off your feet, and have a few laughs. One of the providers of those laughs was Phil Kramer, a little comedian with a Brooklyn accent and a high nasal voice. One day, Phil was auditioning for an important radio director, Bill Wolfe. Phil went through his audition material and Mr. Wolfe said, "Ah…that's good, Phil. Ah…do you have any other voices you can do?"

Phil replied, "Well, ah kin tolk up heah like dis, or, ah kin tolk down heah like dis." The entire line was delivered on one note in Phil's high, nasal voice.

On another occasion, Phil came to the Actor's Lounge and found it practically empty. He turned to me and asked, "Where is evahbody?"

I said, "Well, it's Ash Wednesday. Maybe they went to St. Pat's Cathedral to have ashes put on their foreheads."

Phil said, "Oh? I didn't git dah call."

If Phil ever saw you do anything on television, no matter how small or insignificant, he would rush up and say, "Hey, Terry! I saw you on da Pinky Lee Show. Nice comeback!"

In those early days of television, all the shows were "live." The teleprompter hadn't been invented yet, nor had tape. On occasion, mistakes were made, and you—the viewing public—got to see them. For instance, a stagehand walking through the middle of the "Robert Montgomery Show" carrying a ladder was a sight that caused the person sitting beside you to ask, "Who the hell was that?"

And who will ever forget Betty Furness, fighting a losing battle with a refrigerator door that refused to open?

On another occasion, an attractive lady presenter was telling us why we should switch to Lux soap. You could see the panic in her eyes when she forgot her lines; then she fortuitously fainted right on camera.

A male announcer hit upon an even more ingenious escape hatch. When he forgot his lines, he stopped talking but kept his lips moving. People in the control room were going crazy. When they found out what he'd done, they wanted to lynch him. Now remember, this happened in the Fabulous Fifties. Had it happened in the eighties, we'd have read his lips the way President Bush taught us to do.

I got my comeuppance with a Muriel Cigar commercial. When I arrived at the studio, lines already learned, the director gave me a slightly revised version of the commercial. He asked me if I wanted cue cards, and I said, "No, I can handle it." And while I did handle the cigar very well, it was the lines that gave me problems. When I got into trouble, I took a big drag off my cigar, blew out a cloud of smoke, looked lovingly at my Muriel, said something complimentary about it, and the thirty seconds were up. I can't say it was a good commercial. On the other hand, it wasn't a disaster. At least I didn't faint! Then, I discovered you can write words on a cigar with a ballpoint pen, and my worries were over.

Do you remember those early days of TV when we could smoke on camera? Yes, and drink on camera. I'm speaking of commercials. I can't tell you how much Mogen David wine I drank on a show called "Dollar a Second" starring Jan Murray. Mogen David was a kosher wine, so the people on the show took to calling me "Terry O'Solomon."

I used to hold up a glass of wine as though I were toasting and say, "Mogen David, the home sweet home wine like Grandma used to make." Then, down the hatch. It tasted sweet and syrupy. I got the job because the announcer before me went through the entire rehearsal without ever tasting the wine. On the show—live, mind you—he took a drink of Mogen David, was surprised by the taste, got some of it caught in his vocal cords, and went into the Red Skelton bit. Have you ever seen Red Skelton doing

Commuter of tomorrow in his personal helicopter, c. 1958

his "Guzzler's Gin" commercial? After a swig of liquid fire, he tries to speak, but nothing comes out.

Well, everyone thought it was funny except Mr. Mogen David, who threatened to cancel the show. The account executive, in desperation, asked, "Who can drink anything and smile?" Someone said, "Terry O'Sullivan!" And that's how I became the voice of Mogen David wine. I drank Mogen David on the rocks, Mogen David Longfellows, Mogen David in tea, and Mogen David on ice cream. Hey—it's not bad on ice cream!

My first summer in New York City was long, hot, and not too rewarding. But near the end of August, I picked up my first show. It was called "Big Town," a new TV series, starring Pat McVey. I played the nephew of a precinct boss, and my girlfriend was played by Grace Kelly. Yes, the lovely lady who became Princess Grace. At that time, Grace Kelly and I were two Irish actors grateful to have a one-time shot on a new series. Somehow it never crossed my mind that she would some day be a big star, and if someone had said, "Grace Kelly will someday be a princess," I'd have said, "Aw, come on!"

She was beautiful and was a very good actress, but New York City could boast of quite a few in that category. How can you tell which actress will become a star? It's like trying to pick the winning horse at the Kentucky Derby. I'm not very good at that, either.

In the play in which we were involved, Grace and I got into an argument, which wound up with my slapping her. Well, it was in the script, so I let her have it. This right hand of mine could be the only hand that ever slapped Grace Kelly—on or off the stage. She was a lady.

About a month later, I ran into Grace on Sixth Avenue and we had coffee at a little delicatessen and discussed our careers, as actors do. After that, I only saw her on TV, in movies, or in magazines. It was like watching an eagle fly. Higher and higher.

Brand new TV show ideas were proliferating in the fifties. Here's an example: I won an audition that called for an actor/ announcer. The show was "Famous Women of History" and it starred Eva Gabor. It went like this: The minute Eva got on camera, she started taking off her clothes, assisted by her maid. When she got down to her slip, or thereabouts, she started putting on the costume of the famous woman she was portraying, talking all the while. I can assure you, this opening scene was an attention getter!

The episode I remember most, and for good reason, was Cleopatra. I played Marc Antony, off camera. The camera never left Eva's pretty face, except when I did the commercials for Gayla Velvet Tip Bobby Pins. These were bobby pins that had their sharp little ends dipped in plastic, so you wouldn't scratch your delicate scalp when you stuck them in your hair. At that time, it was a new concept for bobby pins.

In Eva's closing remarks for the Cleopatra show, she said, "I do vant to tank Terry O'Sullivan for doing such a vunderful job as Cleopatra."

Cleopatra? Did she say Cleopatra?

I couldn't believe my ears. A few moments later when the little red light went off, people literally fell out of the control room—laughing and reaffirming my brilliant performance as Cleopatra!

I must say it was fun to work with Eva. She suffered so beautifully and vas so Hungarian. Sometimes we rehearsed at her home. The phone would ring and she'd say, "Hello, Dahling. I'm exhausted. Ve vere up all night vorking on the script. Now ve're rehearsing. I'll call you later."

Her townhouse, a recent acquisition, was on Fifth Avenue, across the street from Central Park, in the Sixties. Prime property? I'd say creme de la creme. Her mama, Jolie Gabor, advised her that she should buy a house so she'd have a roof over her head—nice roof!

Her boyfriend at this time was Stuart Barthelmes, son of the silent picture star, Richard Barthelmes.

"Famous Women of History" ran for thirteen weeks, then disappeared into the vast vortex of TV shows that didn't quite make it.

My next show was a radio play called "True Detective." Here I played opposite an actress named Jan Miner. Perhaps you know her as Madge the manicurist from TV commercials for Palmolive. In those days she was known as Julie of "Hilltop House," a popular radio soap opera.

I had a déjà vu feeling about Jan, as though we had met before, or I had known someone like her. We were very much at ease in each other's company, so I invited her to have a drink after the show. She said she was busy, but she would love a rain check. A few weeks later, I was having a drink at Cherios, a hangout for actors. Mario, the bartender, placed a martini in front of me.

"Where did this come from?" I asked.

He replied, "Compliments of Jan Miner."

I looked in the dining room and there sat a smiling Jan Miner. So I joined her for dinner. I was new in town and she had recently said goodbye to someone.

A couple of weeks later, on a Sunday afternoon, Jan and I were having a cup of tea in her apartment. The phone rang and Jan said, "You answer it."

I replied, "I'm not very good at this."

She said, "Go ahead."

"Okay, but who am I?"

"Donald, my brother."

I answered the phone, "Jan Miner's residence."

A woman's voice asked, "Who is this?"

I chirped right up, "This is Donald, Jan's brother."

"Really?" said the voice, "I'm Jan's mother."

I paused, then said, "Hello, Mother."

And that's how I met my future mother-in-law.

20

Method Acting

ELEVISION, THE BRAND NEW MEDIUM, was creating a revolution in show business. Not since the advent of talking pictures had there been such an upheaval. For instance, radio actors, who had acquired the art of focusing all their acting skills in their voices, were now called upon to coordinate body movement with voice to achieve a fully integrated, visual performance. This called for some heavy retooling. It was generally agreed that the best place to accomplish this transition was in an acting class. In 1951 most acting classes in New York City were teaching some variation of "the Method."

Method acting demanded real tears; crocodile tears were not good enough. You, the actor, must feel grief. Then your audience will be moved. Sometimes the camera comes in very close. It wants to see what you are feeling. So how does an actor set about feeling grief? In method acting, you are taught to use recall. This is a personal thing. You think back to a time in your life when your tears flowed. For me, the memory of my father's funeral would produce a lump in the throat. I would close my eyes. I could hear the church bell tolling, slowly, ominously. I could see the vaulted interior of St. Andrew's Church with its statues and its stained glass windows, the coffin placed near the altar. I could feel the great abyss that separates the living from the dead, and grief would engulf me.

Many actors felt rather skeptical about "the Method." It was the subject of much discussion and debate. Some actors absolutely refused to have anything to do with method acting. Marlon Brando, a graduate of Sandy Meisner's Actor Studio, was probably the best known method actor. He was great.

Jan and I felt that some method was better than no method, so we joined David Alexander's acting class. For openers, David gave what seemed to us a rather bizarre assignment. We were to visit the zoo in Central Park, choose whichever animal took our fancy, imitate that animal's movements, give the animal an action or need, and perform same in front of the class.

So off we went to the zoo. I decided I would be an elephant, using my right arm as the trunk, swaying rhythmically as elephants are wont to do. His need was to be loved. Jan chose an ostrich and held an arm up, her hand representing the ostrich head. We both picked up some laughs when we did this exercise for the class. The good part was that we found ourselves so busy imitating the animal and pursuing its need that we didn't have time to feel self-conscious. Then a young actor got up to perform; his animal was a python and his action to steal the pearls. He came slithering up over a desk and Jan whispered, "Hey, he's good." She was right. He was good. He is good. His name is Jack Lemmon.

We attended David's class for a couple of months. Then a friend of Jan's, Don Richardson, decided to start a class in acting. Don at this time was directing the TV show, "I Remember Mama." Most of the dozen or so students in this class were soap opera actors, currently performing in radio. Jan at this time was Julie of "Hilltop House," a radio soap opera. Do you remember Ma Perkins? Who could ever forget Ma, the lumberyard, and Shuffle, her faithful employee? Ginny Payne played Ma. When she started the role, she was a young woman. Thirty years later, when the show ended in the mid-fifties, she could have played Ma on TV with very little makeup. Ginny Payne was in our class. A very warm personality.

Don taught that, in each scene, an actor had to select two elements: his emotion, what he feels; and his action, that which he is trying to achieve. Suppose you are a thief and your action is to steal the pearls. Normally, you would choose fear as your emotion. But if you were playing a kleptomaniac, you might chose lust as your emotion, because stealing turns you on.

Warren Parker and I did the gravedigger scene from *Hamlet* in the manner of Laurel and Hardy. I played Hardy. My emotion was greed and my action was to get him to do the work, meantime sneaking sips of wine from our bottle. The results were quite hilarious.

Don had a unique talent. In his personal life, he could turn tragedy into comedy. During the time we attended his class, he was going through a difficult divorce. Jan and I would join him for dinner in Greenwich Village, then go to his apartment to hear about the latest battle in the ongoing

Terry and Jan, c. 1957

war of sparring lawyers, battling principals, frozen assets, and massive frustration.

After one of the aforementioned sessions, I asked Jan, "Why were we laughing so hard?"

She replied, "Because Don is a funny man."

He was also a good teacher; we stayed in his class four years.

Don and I had two hobbies that bound us together as buddies: fishing and matrimony. To feel a heavy tug at the end of a line and to see a bent, wiggling fishing rod gave us a deep, primitive thrill. Then we both had the irrepressible optimism of romantics. No matter how horrible, no matter how financially disastrous the end of a marriage might be, it was only a matter of time before we would once again find life's meaning in some lovely lady's eyes. The color was optional; the message came through blue eyes as clearly as through brown. The message: "Your happiness lies in my hands. Trust me. I will cherish you always."

Like Don Quixote, our actions might appear strange to the casual observer, but from our point of view we were simply pursuing our destinies.

To sum it up, it is my belief that Don caught more fish than I, while I caught more wives than he.

In my unrelenting pursuit of romance, I eventually acquired six wives. Somehow, the scope of my activity didn't occur to me until I visited the home of a friend, Jim Scott. Jim collected beer mugs, the big kind with faces on them. Along a wall was a three-shelf display case divided in the middle. At the top was the regal visage of Henry VIII, looking sternly from the side of a beer mug. Under him were his six wives, now attached to beer mugs rather than to their king.

I thought, "That's me! Six wives!" It wasn't until I saw this beer mug display that I comprehended the extent of my matrimonial activity. Six wives! I go from day to day, from one income tax filing to the next, and am not really aware of what I did last year or the year before, but the cumulative effect can be startling.

In the end, life doesn't change much from century to century. There are always wars; there is always romance. But, alas, sometimes romance turns into warfare. Amen.

21

"Search for Tomorrow"

*O*NE DAY MY AGENT sent me to audition for a soap opera. An actress and I read a scene in front of a small group of people—the writers, producer, director, agency rep. When we finished, the director asked the group if they had any questions. There were no questions, so he thanked me for coming. As I closed the door, I said to myself, "Oh, well, many are called but few are chosen. Forget that one!" I was really surprised when I got a call the following day to appear on "Search for Tomorrow." Then I received a call for the next week.

The calls were scattered at first. Then they came with greater frequency, until it occurred to me that Arthur Tate, the part I was playing, was becoming the leading man. A romance was developing between Arthur and Joanne. We looked good together—as though we belonged. As one fan wrote, "Dear Arthur: When I watch you make love to Joanne, it's hard for me to believe that you are married to Jan Miner."

I wrote back to my fan. "Thank you for the really nice compliment. Each day, on 'Search for Tomorrow,' we strive to make fantasy a reality."

Apparently we were successful, because for three consecutive years, we won favorite Daytime Drama Actor and Actress Awards.

Once we played a love scene on the front porch steps. It was a summer night with moon shadows, and crickets softly in the background. Very romantic. Then I did something an actor should never do. I stepped out of my fantasy world and into the real world of Terry O'Sullivan. I said to myself, "Hey, this scene is really playing great, isn't it?" I should have said, "wasn't it." I had broken my concentration. Now it was my turn to speak, but I couldn't for the life of me think of what I was supposed to say. So we sat there in the moonlight, listening to the crickets chirp.

Finally, Joanne said, "What are you thinking about, Arthur?" Her question broke the log jam in my brain and I remembered my line. It was, "I was thinking how quiet it is." It had been very quiet. For quite a spell. Joanne's question saved the day. Remember, this was in the early 1950s, before teleprompters and tape had been invented.

We actors always tried to help each other if we could, and for some insane reason there were times when I seemed to know the other actor's lines better than my own. Once when Joanne was in serious trouble in our story, our lawyer, Nathan Walsh, called an important meeting with the Tates—Arthur and Joanne—and our good friends, the Bergmans—Stu and Marge. Nathan did most of the talking, since he was outlining the strategy he planned for the upcoming trial. Nathan was presenting his plan like a skillful lawyer until all of a sudden he forgot his lines, at which point he turned to Stu and said, "Stu, do you remember what I told you about this?"

Stu's eyes widened as his brain went into overdrive, and he said, "Ah, yeah, Nathan, I think you said you were going to hire a private detective to tail Higbee."

Nathan was back on track and continued his lawyer talk. However, a little farther down the lane he drew another blank. Again he turned to Stu with a question, "Stu, do you recall what I told you about this?"

Stu looked frantic as he racked his brain. Then he blurted out, "No, Nathan, I don't."

Luckily I did, so I came to the rescue with, "Didn't you say you had discovered something about Mortimer Higbee's past?"

Nathan was back on track and stayed there 'til the end of the scene.

When this episode was over, we actors held a meeting in the dressing room and decided that our show should have a new name. Instead of "Search for Tomorrow," we would call it "Search for Lines." Normally our shows went quite smoothly, but once in a while we got into trouble.

It seemed to me that about once a year we would wind up in court. This time it was because of Joanne. She had been falsely accused of murder by the villainous Mortimer Higbee. In truth, we actors loved to go to court because the lawyers had most of the lines. Some days we would just sit in the courtroom listening to the proceedings and occasionally we'd do a reaction for the camera. Even when we were called on to testify, the lawyers had to initiate the questions. As a soap opera actor, you spend your life learning lines—literally.

Our work week went like this: scripts for the upcoming week would arrive in the mail on Thursday or Friday. I would quickly skim through them to evaluate the workload for the week ahead. If I were deeply

RADIO MIRROR

March 30, 1955

Dear Terry:

Heartiest congratulations!

In its Eighth Annual Awards Poll, and the only nationwide
poll of its kind, the readers of TV RADIO MIRROR have
voted you their "favorite daytime drama actor on TV
for 1954-55" for your portrayal of Arthur Tate on
"Search for Tomorrow."

May TV RADIO MIRROR, containing the complete awards
story, will be on sale April 7. I will be deeply grateful
if this information is kept confidential until that date.

Best wishes and, once again, congratulations!

Sincerely,

Shell Science
MACFADDEN PUBLICATIONS, INC.

P.S. Our readers gave the gold medal to "Search for
Tomorrow" as their "favorite daytime drama on TV."

Letter from TV Radio Mirror *announcing poll results*

involved in the current story line, I might have four or five shows to do that week. When that happened, I would cancel any social obligations and start learning lines. Usually I did two or three shows a week.

Our rehearsal was held in the banquet room of the Knickerbocker Hotel on East 56th Street. The rehearsal call was 8:00 A.M. Some glamorous actresses didn't look very glamorous at 8:00 A.M., and some performers discovered they didn't know their lines as well as they thought they did.

The favorite excuse for flubbing lines: "I swear I was bedroom perfect last night."

The director's reply, "But we can't shoot the scene in your bedroom, now can we?"

At 10:00 A.M. we would move to Liederkrantz Hall on East 58th Street where we did our show. In the early days of TV, all sorts of studio space was commandeered for this burgeoning industry. Liederkrantz Hall had originally belonged to a German singing society. The walls were soundproof and the ceilings high, perfect for TV. Our first stop at Liederkrantz was makeup. This was the nicest moment of the day. I would sit there relaxed, eyes closed, while Joy Lang, our makeup girl, applied makeup to my fevered brow with her cool, damp sponge. Then into the studio where camera shots must be lined up. Much like a Brownie camera, the picture must be composed and focused before you click the shutter.

In the studio are three mobile cameras operated by three cameramen. Let's take a simple scene where Joanne and Arthur are sitting at the kitchen table talking after breakfast—drinking coffee, of course. Camera Two will take the wide shot of the two of us, seated at the table. Camera One will have a closeup of Jo's face, Camera Three will have a closeup of Arthur. The director, Dan Levin, in the control room, calls the shots. When he says, "Take one," viewers at home will see a closeup of Joanne. When he says, "Take two," you see a closeup of Arthur. "Take three," you see the two of us seated.

This is a classic example of a simple scene in the kitchen. The director marks his script like a music score; therefore the actors can't ad lib. When Arthur says, "Well, Jo, guess I'd better get to work," the director says "Take two." Camera Two will be focused on a wide shot and you will see Arthur and Joanne stand up and walk to the door. Camera One will be positioned for the good-bye kiss. All of this camera procedure must be blocked out and marked. Then comes dress rehearsal. After dress, the director gives his notes to the actors like, "Don't move on the good-bye kiss; the camera is in close. Before you say 'Well, Jo, guess I'd better get

Terry O'Sullivan and Mary Stuart of "Search for Tomorrow," c. 1954

to work,' let us see that you are worried about the meeting you are going to attend this morning." After notes, we would have maybe half an hour to firm up some lines and think about the director's critique, and then we were "on live" from coast to coast, and good luck!

Accidents can, and on occasion do, happen. One time Joanne was waiting for me to come home from work. She took out a favorite recording and placed it on a console. The console had been placed on wooden blocks so it would be more visible and make a better picture. She was dreamily dancing to the music when I entered. I walked over to Jo to give her a kiss. Camera Two was moving in for a closeup. Camera Two pushed a bit too close and pushed the console off its blocks. It fell to the floor with a crash that would have awakened Rip Van Winkle. This happened on the show. I thought, is there anything I can say to explain that noise? Then I thought, do you know what your line is? Try saying that. We got through the scene, but the values, the romantic nuances went with the crash. When shows were presented live, you had one chance to do it right and no chance of going back, ever.

Danger tends to make believers of us all. Most soldiers try to get in touch with "whatever Gods there be" the night before a big battle. Kirby Puckett, the slugger, crossed himself before he stepped up to the plate to slam one into the bleachers.

As actors in the early days of TV, we were like tightrope walkers who worked without a net. There was always a chance that we might forget a line. Have you ever attempted to introduce two friends and have your brain short circuit, blocking out a familiar name? On occasion, that is what happens to an actor. He knows the line, but it hides from him.

This kind of insecurity causes actors to turn to prayer or superstition for help in their upcoming performances. About five minutes before the little red light would go on in the studio, signifying "you are on the air and nine million pairs of eyes are watching you," we actors on "Search for Tomorrow" would go through a ritual which we performed religiously—before each show. It was called "Good Luck Time." Joanne insisted that the rite be performed the exact same way each time. The manner in which you wished her good luck the first time you were on the show must be repeated in the exact same way forever after. For instance, I would shake hands with Joanne, look into her eyes, say "Good luck," then kiss her on the neck.

At the end of this "Good Luck Time" ceremony, Joanne and Marge would position themselves about ten feet apart, open their arms wide, rush toward each other, embrace, then whisper something in each other's ear. What did they whisper? We never found out.

IN THE ANNUAL AWARDS POLL CONDUCTED BY

TV RADIO MIRROR

AMERICAN TV AUDIENCES HAVE CHOSEN

Terry O'Sullivan

AS THEIR

FAVORITE DAYTIME DRAMA ACTOR

FOR HIS ROLE AS ARTHUR TATE IN

SEARCH FOR TOMORROW

PUBLISHER
MACFADDEN PUBLICATIONS

EDITOR
TV RADIO MIRROR

Award certificate from TV Radio Mirror

I, too, had my secret ritual. I would say to myself, "Help me, angels. Make me a harp that his hand can touch me; make me a flute that his breath can pass through me." The concept for my prayer came from *The Prophet* by Kahlil Gibran.

Did this ritualistic ceremony help? You be the judge. "Search for Tomorrow" was broadcast five times a week, Monday through Friday, fifty-two weeks a year, for thirty-five years. Joanne, Mary Stuart, was there for all those shows. She was there for the very first show; she was there when the final curtain fell. What a record. I found "tomorrow" after twelve years. But twelve years is not what you'd call a shabby run.

Soap operas are hard, fast work for all concerned—writers, actors, directors, and cameramen. Think of it this way: doing a half-hour show five times a week equals 2½ hours of playing time, subtract the commercials, and you still have a feature-length film. Has anyone ever shot a feature film in five days? No! Not even Orson Welles could do that.

At some time in the Fabulous Fifties, Harry Reasoner hosted a talk show. The subject for this particular day's discussion was "Are Actors Schizophrenic?" In other words, do they sometimes get their own character mixed up with the character they are playing, especially when they perform the same role over a period of time? He cited a movie where Ronald Coleman played a Shakespearean actor who became famous for his portrayal of Othello. Every night on stage, Ronald Coleman, as Othello, would strangle his wife, Desdemona. But one night, offstage, when he was in his cups, he attempted to strangle his real wife.

For the discussion, Harry Reasoner had invited a group of soap opera actors—people who had played the same role over a period of time. He asked Barbara Becker if she thought actors were schizophrenic—did she, for instance, find herself taking on some of the characteristics of the part she played? Barbara replied, "I certainly hope not, because Julia is a drunk and a real bitch."

Then he turned to me and said, "What about you, Terry, how do you feel about yourself in relation to Arthur Tate—the part you play?"

I replied quite simply, "I am Arthur Tate." My answer got a big laugh, but as far as I was concerned, it was true. In approaching a scene, I didn't ask myself, "How would Arthur Tate feel about this?" I said, "How do I feel about this?" and played the scene from that point of view. I don't know whether Terry became like Arthur or if Arthur became like Terry, but somewhere along the way, we must have merged.

Schizophrenic? Could be. Remind me *not* to play Othello.

What is it we are seeking in this life? Isn't it recognition? Well, maybe not everybody. Rodney Dangerfield is seeking respect. So let's say we are seeking respect and recognition.

As a soap opera actor, you may not always get respect, but you will get recognition. The minute you get out of New York City, it starts. Stop at a Howard Johnson's for lunch, and the waitresses start getting excited, whispering to each other. Finally, one asks the big question: "Are you Arthur Tate?"

When you say "Yes," you may have a few autographs to sign.

One night I was driving into New York City from our New Hampshire farm. I got sleepy, so I pulled over to the side of the Merritt Parkway and went to sleep. I was awakened by a bright light shining in my eyes. Then a stern voice said, "Who are you?"

Without a moment's hesitation, I replied, "Arthur Tate."

The flashlight went out, and the voice said, "I'll be damned. Wait 'til I tell my wife that I found Arthur Tate sleeping alongside the Merritt Parkway!"

I was looking at a highway patrolman. I said, "Lots of women recognize me, but it's rather unusual for a man to know who I am."

Now he was as friendly as a puppy dog. He said, "I work at night, so I have breakfast at noon, and my wife and I always watch 'Search for Tomorrow.' Ahh—could I have your autograph? Just to prove that I met you."

As I drove on into New York City, I began to think about Harry Reasoner and that word, "schizophrenic," and how, without even thinking, I had said to the highway patrolman, "I'm Arthur Tate." It was the right thing to say, but the word schizophrenic kept coming back to haunt me.

Don Knotts and Lee Grant appeared on "Search for Tomorrow" for about a six-month run, playing brother and sister. Both of them became big names, but at this time they were two free-lance actors. In our story, Don had gone through a very traumatic experience which left him unable to speak. What a nice break for Don—he didn't have to learn any lines! However, this meant that an actor playing a scene with him had to do all the talking. All Don could do was shake his head, yes or no. I can tell you it was a happy day in my life when the psychiatrist unlocked Don's tongue and restored his ability to speak.

I remember saying to him, "Now, Don, you're going to find out what soap opera is all about."

He said, "What is soap opera all about, Terry?"

I said, "It's all about learning lines."

Don gave me that funny smile of his and said, "Yeah, I guess you're right."

After Don left our show, he went into the Broadway play *No Time for Sergeants,* and from there to "The Andy Griffith Show" on TV, where he played the deputy sheriff, Barney.

Once again I failed to recognize a rising star. However, a soap opera is the worst place in the world to show off your ability to make people laugh, and Don Knotts can surely do that!

As we go through life, we all have unforgettable moments. I had one such on "Search for Tomorrow." It occurred during my convalescence from a heart attack. Dr. Moore, played by the actor Marty Brooks, made a house call to check on my recovery. First, he took my temperature. Then, in a very professional manner, he wrapped the blood pressure gizmo around my upper arm. Then he started squeezing the little bulb, and he

kept on squeezing the little bulb until the pressure on my arm was inde-
scribable. I thought, "If he gives that bulb one more squeeze, I'm going to
kick him—nine million TV viewers or not!" He must have noticed that my
eyes were bulging out of their sockets, for he stopped just in the nick of
time! Talk about working under pressure—that was really it!

Each year, *TV Radio Mirror* magazine would conduct a poll. Ballots
were printed in the magazine, so the readers could vote for their favorite
TV actors.

One of the most thrilling moments of my life was when I was notified
that I had won the Favorite Daytime Drama Actor Award. I won that award
for three consecutive years: 1953, 1954, and 1955. Being a celebrity was
a heady experience. Wherever I went, I was recognized and often called
upon to give an autograph.

All of those endless hours spent learning lines paid off handsomely in
that priceless commodity called recognition.

22

Jan's Farm in New Hampshire

*I*N THE SHADOW of the White Mountains lies a beautiful lake. The Indians named it Winnipesaukee. On a peninsula that thrusts south into the clear waters of Lake Winnipesaukee, down a country lane, then on your left, is Jan's farm. A bit of nostalgia left over from another age, with its white house, red barn, two apple trees, three large maples, and those wonderful stone walls: paralleling the roads, edging the fields, disappearing into the woods, and joining the neighbor's walls, to divide much of New England into tidy fields.

Today, trees, the original occupants of the New England soil, have quietly re-established themselves in many of the unused fields. These new forests smell of pine, but are a mix of pine, maple, birch, and oak. When September nights grow frosty, a glorious mixture of color erupts in the forest; green, red, and yellow, with touches of russet here and there. Autumn in New Hampshire is spectacular.

Those stone walls that edge the fields are called dry walls, because no cement or mortar is used in their construction. The weight of the stones and their skillful placement, one on top of the other, are the elements that hold these primitive structures together. However, as Robert Frost pointed out in his poem, "Mending Walls," each spring they need a bit of tending to. Frost heaves, the unbelievable strength water exerts when it turns into ice, clumsy hunters in pursuit of deer or partridge, livestock reaching for a morsel of green, can cause stones to loosen and fall. The walls remain today, though a bit tumbled and neglected looking.

Something deep inside me responded to this New Hampshire farm, as though I had been there before or seen it in a dream.

Jan's farm in New Hampshire, 1957

Farms were not something new in my life. My home was just two blocks from the city limits—where the city ended and the country began. This rural setting enabled me to have a horse and a flock of chickens.

Also, Timothy A. O'Sullivan, the grain man, kept us current on the condition of winter wheat in Kansas, and whether the outlook for the corn crop in Iowa was bullish or bearish. With such a background, I considered myself a quasi-farmer or a citified cowboy, quite capable of administering a bit of tender loving care to a somewhat neglected farm.

I repaired walls, mowed fields, and contracted to have the house restored. It became my magnificent obsession. In retrospect, it was a good counterbalance to the nerve game I played in New York City called soap opera. One actor summed it up beautifully, when he said, "My God, in soap opera, every day is opening night." Well put, fellow actor. We never became too familiar with our lines.

In that red barn I mentioned was a Ford tractor complete with a cutting blade for mowing and a plow for turning over the soil. I thought, "I'll plow that small field behind the house. No big deal, after all, I once plowed a half section of land in western Kansas."

I quickly learned what Horace Greeley meant when he said, "Go west, young man. Go west." After generations of cultivation, there were still stones in that good earth. As one New Hampshire farmer observed, "They seem to grow like weeds. It's the one crop you can depend on."

In this field were two huge, iceberg-like rocks whose tops protruded a bit through the earth. I skirted around those monsters, as had the farmers who preceded me, but once, when I was looking back at my furrow, I slid the transmission of the tractor up onto one of those rock protrusions, and one wheel of my tractor spun helplessly in the air. It took much jacking and blocking before I could continue my plowing.

Terry with (left to right) Colleen, Jan, Molly, and Kathleen

All was going smoothly when suddenly the tractor came to an abrupt halt. The plow had come in contact with a rock of sufficient girth to freeze my tractor rig to the spot. I fooled around with the lift and managed to move the rock up out of its earthy bed. Now it needed to be dragged over to the edge of the field and added to the stone wall.

After my plowing experience, I understood why most of New England was returning to forest. In the Midwest, plowing a field was much like driving a car down a country road. There were no impediments.

The people of New Hampshire fascinated me. They didn't believe in wasting words or money. Once in the merry month of May, Jan and I journeyed up to the farm for a couple of days. On Sunday, we had been

Terry, Jan, and Terry's daughters bringing in the hay

basking in the warm spring sun in our bathing suits. Monday morning we woke to find a couple of inches of snow on the ground. The poor robins were having a hell of a time trying to rustle up some breakfast on a snow-covered lawn. A favorite expression of the natives was, "If yuh don't like our weathah, wait a minute." An "er" at the end of a word was always pronounced "ah"—the way President Kennedy spoke.

We headed back to New York that snowy morning in May, but stopped at a quaint little country store with a gas pump out front. A slender grandmother wearing a purple sweater stepped briskly out of the store and greeted us with, "Short summah, wadn't it?" Violent weather and quick climate changes were a way of life in New Hampshire.

"Up the rud a piece from our fam" lived Joe Leach and his wife. Big Joe was a Paul Bunyan type fellow. He was known as the man who'd been struck by lightning and survived. "Aye-yuh. He was milkin' a cow in his bahn when the lightnin' bolt hit. Kilt the cow, deadah than hell and most nearly electrocuted Joe. Spent several yeahs in an institution, but he recovered. Wouldn't go so far as to say he's good as new, but then who is?"

The first time I took my daughters up to visit the farm, Mother Nature put on a midsummer display of lightning and thunder that had the girls trembling in their sandals. This sort of ferocious weather doesn't occur in L.A. I assured them, "Don't worry, girls. There's nothing to be afraid of."

Terry with daughters (left to right) Molly, Kathleen, and Colleen

They were following me closely as I shut a window in the living room, and right on cue, as if it had been rehearsed, the god of thunder threw a bolt of lightning into Annie Bosson's field, right across the road, two hundred feet away. We saw it hit the earth. The crash of thunder was enormous and simultaneous. The girls screamed. I almost joined them. I'd never been that close to a lightning strike. How could Joe Leach have survived a bolt like that? His must have been a few megawatts smaller. I don't think my daughters ever totally trusted me again. "Don't worry, girls. There's nothing to be afraid of." Ben Franklin was a brave man, sending kites up to capture lightning.

I was born during one of those wild Midwest thunderstorms that arrive in July. Because of the storm, the doctor was delayed. Luckily, my grandmother Nesch was there, because my mother had an enormous urge to go sit on the toilet. My grandmother screamed, "No, Amy, don't do that. The child might be born in the toilet." Wouldn't that have been an ignoble way to begin my journey, born in a toilet?

I arrived before the doctor got there. The only time in my life that I've been early for an appointment.

23

I Believe in Santa Claus

Christmas comes but once a year,
And when it comes it brings good cheer,
And when it goes it leaves us here,
And what'll we do for the rest of the year?
    —Cornelius A'Nonymous, an Irish Poet

*C*OME, COME, CORNELIUS, surely you know the answer to that question. You start preparing for next year's Christmas immediately. And if you hold steady on, you might be ready when those silver bells jingle on a frosty night.

The celebration of Christmas grows greater by the year. Macy's parade in New York with enormous animated balloons, the lighting ceremony in Kansas City's Plaza, the Santa Claus parade in Hollywood, where Santa sweats in his fur-trimmed winter wear while his reindeer pant for a few cool flakes of snow.

The last few days before the main event become frantic, with back-to-back cocktail parties interspersed with shopping sprees. To all the aforementioned add career activity. I had been working more than usual in "Search for Tomorrow." The result was sheer exhaustion, which for me generally culminates in a virus of some sort. To avoid this Christmas bonus, Jan and I, along with her mother, headed north out of the plague-ridden big city toward the crisp, sparkling air of New Hampshire.

Here I must take a moment to speak of Jan's mother, Mrs. Ethyl Miner of Boston, a remarkable lady. I dubbed her the world's oldest living ingénue, for she had not matured in the normal manner. She giggled easily and chattered endlessly, much like a high school girl.

"God knows I've tried, Santa!"

When we started this journey, I must admit I was not in a good mood. When I get tired, I become cranky. So to pass the time, I was delivering a diatribe on how a beautiful holiday like Christmas had been turned into a nightmare by greed and excess.

When we reached the Massachusetts Turnpike, it started to snow. I said, "Okay, ladies, that does it. We are stopping at Ye Publick House in Sturbridge, where we shall spend the night." There were no objections, so I pulled into the driveway of this wonderful old New England Inn, which had provided comfort to weary travellers since the year 1776.

We managed to get a table in the tap room, near the fireplace, an enormous stone structure left over from another age. It was called a walk-in fireplace, because you could literally walk into it. It was aglow with burning logs. The dinner was delicious. Still, I persisted in my Scrooge mood. In fact, I went so far as to say, "Some day I hope to play Scrooge, in 'A Christmas Carol.' I understand what motivates him. When I say, "Bah, humbug!" children will frantically clutch their mother's skirts and ask, 'Who is that awful man, Mommy?' "

We trudged upstairs silently. The rooms were delightfully old fashioned. Two crisp, red apples on the chest of drawers brought a smile of appreciation. I was taking off a shoe when the damnedest thing happened. Out of nowhere came the voices of carolers singing "Silent Night." I mean really singing "Silent Night" like a glee club. I dropped my shoe and walked to the window—presumably to see the carolers. Actually, I didn't want Jan to see my face. Scrooges don't weep; they say, "Bah, humbug!" I couldn't see the carolers, but what I did see only intensified the lump in my throat. Across the snowy commons were half a dozen New England homes of traditional white clapboard, each with a lighted Christmas tree in the front yard. Two street lamps revealed light snow sparkling as it fell. Thank heavens the carolers started to sing "Jingle Bells," or I'd surely have started to shed tears. I turned back to Jan and said, "Have you heard the good news? Scrooge is dead! Long live Christmas! I still believe in Santa Claus. I may not in the morning, but tonight I do."

And so to bed. While visions of sugarplums danced in our heads.

HOTEL PIERRE

Cotillion room

STANLEY MELBA
presents

"Music in the Air"

A musical comedy
With book and lyrics by OSCAR HAMMERSTEIN II
Music by
JEROME KERN
with

PHYLLIS ARICK	MARTHE ERROLLE
WILBUR EVANS	TERRY O'SULLIVAN

HARRY SNOW

Adapted and Staged by   *Lighting by*
DOLORES PALLET   LESLIE WHEEL

Musical Arrangements and Orchestra Conducted by
LEE HULBERT

Announcement for Music in the Air

24

Music in the Air

THE FABULOUS FIFTIES were my Golden Age: a soap opera star married to a bright, fun actress.

I once did a play called *The Seven Year Itch* at the Old Log Theater. The itch is a malady that strikes married men after seven or eight years of connubial bliss. The symptoms are a roving eye, a slight fever, and a loss of immunity to pretty girls. In this play, the wife is on vacation. The husband is innocently sitting on the terrace reading *Playboy.* A potted plant falls from the apartment above and smashes on the deck. If the owner of that plant turns out to be Marilyn Monroe, as was the case in the movie, it's advisable to dial 911 and take your temperature while waiting for the rescue squad. Tell them to hurry because the disease can be fatal. Now I digress, but we'll double back; never fear.

My agent, Kooky Kaleen—actually her name was Madelyn, but she was a bit kooky, fun kooky—had a myna bird named Teapu, who spoke rather well—English, that is. When Ms. Kaleen went off for a weekend, she would recruit some of her clients to look after darling little Teapu. "Drop by late afternoon. Feed him, check his water, chat with him." Late one Saturday afternoon I stepped into the office to tend to Teapu. He let out a myna bird squawk, cocked his head, looked at me sharply, and said "What a ham!" I found it a bit unsettling that a myna bird would be so perceptive.

Later, I complained to Ms. Kaleen that never had I been so insulted—by a bird. She said, "I'm working on a deal for you, Terry, and if it comes through, you'll be so happy you'll buy Teapu a new cage."

"What's the deal, Madelyn?"

She told me that the Cotillion Room of Hotel Pierre was going to do a condensed version of *Music in the Air* by Jerome Kern and Oscar Hammerstein. "The part of the producer, Ernst Weber, should be right up your alley." And right up my alley it was. I got it. The Cotillion Room was a class joint with a capital K. I really looked forward to *Music in the Air.*

I had been walking through the tar of "Search for Tomorrow" for some time now, and I needed something new, something to quicken the tempo of a going-nowhere plot and dull lines to be committed to memory.

Too, my marriage seemed anchored in a becalmed sea. Jan had been doing a series of off- and off-off-Broadway plays, where she specialized in playing frumpy old slatterns who wore bird-watcher shoes, bag-lady dresses, and flat hairdos secured by a rubber band. She gloried in looking like something that had just wiggled out of an ash can. A perfect mate for Oscar of Sesame Street. It turned me off, somehow. It shouldn't have, after all. I'm an actor. I know that when you take the makeup off, you take the part off, but she seemed to be obsessed with these old crones.

When the hunchback of Notre Dame is played by a woman—and it will be, an Andrew Lloyd Weber production, likely—Jan Miner will play the part. They'll call her Quasimoda instead of Quasimodo.

Sing a song of hunchbacks, hear the tolling bells.
Notre Dame is calling to drudges and to swells.
She's scaling up a steeple like a spider on its web.
She's dangling from a gargoyle like Harold Lloyd the reb.
Cheers for Quasimoda; let's glorify her name.
Cheers for Quasimoda, for she *is* Notre Dame.

I was afflicted by a virulent strain of boredom that bordered on ennui. *Music in the Air* swept into my life like a breath of spring after a long, hard winter. This was my renaissance, an emergence from the doldrums into a land of bright lights and beautiful music.

I rushed over to Otto Perl's tailor shop and had him measure me for a new tuxedo. No way would I step out in front of that chic crowd of New Yorkers wearing the formal garment that hung limply in my closet.

How I lived through the six-week run of *Music,* I do not know. It must have been on energy generated from excitement. We were scheduled to do two shows a night, at 9:30 and 11:30 P.M. Sometimes the late show was cancelled, thank God, because rehearsal for "Search for Tomorrow" started at 8:30 A.M. I was not too heavily involved in the current story; even so, sleep was a commodity I did not get much of.

A performance of Music in the Air

Is there anything in this world more exhilarating than to read a good review about yourself?

The producer of "Music in the Air," Ernst Weber, is played by Terry O'Sullivan, an accomplished television actor in his cafe debut. He it is who helps make this production one of the best, from the acting standpoint, the Cotillion Room has offered. He makes his mark with dialogue rather than song. Terry has his big chance after the musical has run its course. In a sort of curtain speech, handsome and assured, with some witty, topical puns, he brings on the cast for introductions.

After reading that review, I decided that I wanted to be a musical comedy star. No matter how tired I might feel, when that overture started, I revived like magic. It was glamorous, it was stimulating, not like a dreary soap opera that deals with life's tragedies and frustrations. I swear that some of that drear finds its way into your psyche, just as a musical comedy, on the other hand, injects joy and sparkle into your life.

Yes, I was out of the doldrums—way out—with a fresh breeze filling my sails. New vistas were opening up. New friendships were being formed. The ingénue and I discovered a rapport—we laughed at the same jokes, with the same intensity. In retrospect, I think we might have kept our relationship on a platonic level—you know, play for her and tonic for me—had we not taken that carriage ride.

One January night when snow covered the earth, we decided to explore Central Park in a horse-drawn carriage. I felt as though we were characters in a Tolstoy novel; the snow, the clip-clop of the horses' hooves. Too, it was bitter cold, we were forced to snuggle to survive, and that's when things got out of hand. Sometimes it's a potted plant, sometimes it's a ride through Central Park. When a person is going through their renaissance, these moments seem like a part of the scenario—written by fate, approved by the gods and inevitable! Inevitable? Well, yes, inevitable, damn it!

25

The Losers Club

When Jan and I started talking about getting a divorce, I didn't just talk, I moved, for I remembered my sad experience with Mary. At first she had been agreeable to getting a divorce, then she changed her mind, leaving me in the limbo of being married, but not married, and unable to get a divorce. I didn't want to fall into that trap again. So I made a quick trip to Juarez for a Mexican divorce. Impulsive? Yes.

Do it now. Think about it later. I did precisely that. I got the divorce. Then I woke up with a strange empty feeling in my gut and a big question in my mind: what have I done? What—have—I—done? I had no immediate answer to that question, but as I looked around at my walk-up apartment on East 62nd Street, I had a strong feeling that I had made a rather large mistake.

The apartment was okay, but from my point of view it did have one itsy bitsy flaw: the cooking facilities were in the bathroom. I say facilities—like a coffeepot and hot plate. This unfortunate cuisine location took some of the creativity out of my cooking.

Also, I was alone. Phyllis had picked up a two-month singing engagement in Seattle. I spent a long and lonely day drawing circles in my mind, always arriving back at the point of beginning, then stupidly setting off again.

Late that afternoon, it occurred to me that I should get the hell out of my depressing apartment. I had spotted a bar down on Lexington Avenue called the Knucklehead. I felt I had something in common with the Knucklehead and we should get acquainted, so I gave up circling and honed in on an objective.

The first thing I saw as I entered the bar was a familiar face. It was Ed Kenner, an ad agency man. Ed directed the TV commercials for Herbert Taryton cigarettes. I had recently auditioned for him. He looked like an ad man: tall, slender, strong jaw, glasses. He welcomed me like a long-lost friend. Already I felt better. Since we had last seen each other, he had lost his job and I had lost my wife. Then he told me about a club that had recently been formed from patrons of the Knucklehead. It was called the Losers Club. To be eligible for membership, you must have lost something or someone that was very important to you. I was eligible, so I joined on the spot. I was overjoyed. I'd found a beautiful watering hole in my neighborhood peopled with kindred spirits. I congratulated Ed when I learned he was president of the Losers. He in turn congratulated me on having the foresight and fortitude to join.

Ed gave me a brief rundown of the members. Henry, another ad man; Charlotte, who had lost heavily in a game called hearts; Lionel, a copywriter; and others. Madison Avenue folk forcibly moved to Lexington Avenue where they could search for the next rung. Now when I was depressed or lonely, I could trot down to the Knucklehead and commiserate with a fellow loser. During my period of adjustment, I kept no booze in my apartment. I didn't trust myself alone with a bottle.

One evening I drifted down to the watering hole, seeking companionship and a Scotch or three. Club member Charlotte was sitting at the bar. Great. This was our chance to get acquainted, swap tragedies, and sip a few. I was much in the mood for all of the above.

Charlotte was thirty-something. Nice looking when she took her glasses off, which she did when she was drinking. The word "average" keeps bubbling up when I seek words to describe her. Brown hair, average height. I enjoyed talking with her because she always seemed genuinely interested in what I was saying.

I learned that Charlotte's "almost marriage" had shipwrecked just short of the altar, leaving her a disillusioned survivor. I could relate to this tragedy in a sincere way, with recalls from my first marriage. Charlotte and I had much in common.

As we floated down a river of Scotch and soda, agleam with ice cubes, Charlotte confided that she thought Ed Kenner was a very attractive man. As her self-appointed-psychiatrist, I pointed out that this was a definite sign of recovery from her unfortunate love affair.

A trip to the men's room brought me to the realization that I was smashed. I said, "Charlotte, I would love to talk to you some more, but I can't drink another drop. Why don't we go to my place? It's only a block away; then we can talk some more. It's so good to find someone I can talk to."

Charlotte graciously accepted my invitation and off we staggered into the darkness, then up three flights of creaky stairs and into my digs.

I still don't know how it happened, but happen it surely did. I tripped on something and fell backward, landing in a sitting position on the glass topped coffee table, which splintered into a bazillion pieces. A moment ago, it had been an attractive coffee table, about three feet square, with a milk-glass top. One second later it was an iron frame surrounding an enormous pile of broken glass. There had been two plates of glass, one on top of the other. How I arose from that mess with but one small cut on my left buttock is the miracle of this or any age. There was a moment of silence. Then the laughter started. I can't tell you how this accident tickled our funny bones—we were hysterical. We laughed so long and hard that we finally flung ourselves down on the bed in utter exhaustion. Then, almost before we realized what was happening, we found ourselves doing that "awful thing."

Then—it's difficult for me to write this, but I feel I must—Charlotte called me Ed. Panting with passion, "Oh, Ed!" she said. "Oooh, E-e-e-ed!" I lacked the courage to point out her unfortunate mistake. Fantasies are an important part of our lives, and we must protect them in ourselves and others.

Just remember, two losers do not a winner make. Amen.

26

The Long-Stemmed Rose

*T*he Knucklehead Bar and my support group, the Losers Club, helped me stagger through the long hot summer. But as August began to edge September, the winds of change started to freshen.

It was that time of day when those who are dependent on alcohol feel an enormous urge. I was seated where I belonged, thinking negative thoughts as a loser is wont to do, when a young lady sat down and ordered a drink. I thought, "This has to be a model: tall, gold-red wavy hair, lovely profile. Hmmm! What the hell! Could it hurt to be neighborly? Buy her a drink."

She seemed so pleased by my friendly gesture that I said "May I?" and sat down beside her. "My name's Terry."

She laughed out loud.

"What's so funny?" I asked.

She replied, "My name's Sherry."

"Well, I'll be damned," said I. "We rhyme! Are you a model?"

"No, I'm a student at the Art Institute."

"The one on 57th Street?"

"Uh huh."

"How about that! I'm an actor. We're in the arts; a toast to artists. May they bring beauty to this world."

Boy meets girl. Well, not quite. Boy was forty-six years old, girl was twenty. More aptly put, mature man meets young lady.

Sherry would have no trouble finding employment in Las Vegas. She was a show-girl type, five-foot-eleven, statuesque, beautiful hair, lovely smile. The bra would have to be padded a bit—no problem. She had the rest. Her home was Winnipeg, Canada. New girl in town. And an artist. How fascinating. I was very fascinated.

There was one thing about Sherry that was quite unusual. She had one light blue eye and one dark blue eye. I had to ask.

She replied, "When I was seven years old, a neighborhood boy threw a rock that hit me in the eye. They had to operate."

"Can you still see out of that eye?"

"Some, but my vision in that eye is impaired."

"May I take you to dinner, Sherry?"

"Sure."

And that is how it began.

The winds of change had not yet blown themselves out. A couple of days later, Madelyn Kaleen called and asked coyly, "Terry, how would you like to do an Off-Broadway play?"

"I'd love to do an Off-Broadway play."

"Well, it's a French play called *Intimate Relations* by Cocteau, and it will be done at the Mermaid Theater on West 42nd Street." Pause.

"Tell me more."

"What if I told you that Jan Miner might play your wife?"

"Oh, my God. Really? Well, she played the part on the stage of life for ten years, so we should be able to act like a couple of marrieds. Let's go for it."

We went for it and we got it.

When I received the news that I had been cast in *Intimate Relations,* I had a dilemma. I really wanted to do this play, but I didn't know what it would be like playing opposite Jan. When rehearsals started, it did feel strange to be playing Jan's husband on stage, having quite recently played Jan's husband on the stage of life. The situation was almost as offbeat as the plot of Cocteau's play, where I, the husband, am having an affair with the ingénue in the afternoon while my son is having a love affair with the young lady at night.

Our dressing room was close to the candy machine. One night, at intermission, I heard a couple of ladies discussing our play. One said, "I thought this play would have a little class. You know, what I mean? Written by Cocteau and all that malarkey."

"Come on, already. This play is about Ninth Avenue here in New York City."

On the subject of family relationships in the theater, I had a theory, to wit: it's difficult to keep your wife happy, and it's difficult to keep your leading lady happy. If ever the two ladies should become one, watch out! Actually, performing with Jan was not a problem, but it did not rekindle in me a longing to return to her. It did bring to mind a couple of lines from *The Rubaiyat* by Omar Khayyam:

> I divorced old barren reason from my bed,
> And took the daughter of wine to spouse.

I thought to myself, "Yes, Terry, that's what you've done. You're a winner!"

But a distant voice replied, "At this moment, you're a winner. Remember what the Losers Club taught you? The Eleventh Commandment is: thou canst not win!"

One night during a performance of *Intimate Relations*, I went up to a peephole in the proscenium. I wanted to see how Sherry was reacting to our show. She seemed to be totally caught up in the plot. Then I noted a young man seated across the aisle from Sherry and one row back. He was mesmerized by that gold red hair. He hadn't the foggiest idea what the actors on the stage were saying. He was only interested in what his eyes were seeing, a pretty girl.

Music in the Air had been a test of my physical endurance, but Cocteau's *Intimate Relations* was even more so. Let's be honest. It was the "trinity" that was killing me. "Search For Tomorrow" with all those lines to learn and deliver, *Intimate Relations* with double-header performances on the weekend, and the Long-Stemmed Rose for whom I had such a passion. To wake up in the morning and see that beautiful red hair scattered on a white pillow—no sunrise could compare.But I was now running on my reserve tank.

I had a meeting with Madelyn Kaleen and her myna bird Teapu. Teapu opened the meeting by asking "Wanna go down Broadway, hmm?"

I said, "No thanks, Teapu. My dear Madelyn, you don't want to lose a perfectly good client, do you?"

"What's the matter, Terry?"

I replied, "I'm suffering from chronic fatigue. I'm becoming exhausted and irritable. I can't give up 'Search,' for that's my wherewithal, I can't give up the long-stemmed rose, for that's my love. Cocteau has got to go, or I may drop dead on the stage of the Mermaid Theater."

So it was agreed that a proper notice would be given. But damned if management didn't beat us to the draw. They tacked up a closing notice. I guess they were tired, too.

Sherry and I celebrated the closing of *Intimate Relations* one Sunday night, but she seemed quiet. Not her usual smiling self.

I asked a couple of times, "What's the matter this evening, Sherry?"

Finally it came out. About a year ago, her parents had sent her to Homewood, a drying-out institution, because of her excessive drinking and mental instability. Oh, Jesus! I might have known there would be something. I didn't say that, but I thought it.

Then I quickly regained my composure and said, "You seem fine now. You drink, but so do I."

She said, "Yes, I am fine, but somehow I felt I should tell you." She had warned me, but it was too late to turn back. She was part of my life now.

Sherry was bright and beautiful. She came from a good family, upper middle class. One brother was an opera singer in Covent Garden. Her other brother was in electronics, married with two children. Then there was Sherry, full of potential but just a trifle screwed up. I, as a man of the world, felt that I could bring this lovely creature into focus and help her realize her true self. A noble undertaking for a white knight.

Sherry and I had a number of things in common. We loved horses. We were both pretty good riders. She rode English; I, Western. She was also a good high jumper. She could scissor right over a barbed-wire fence—an area in which I did not compete. I had a scar on one of my fingers from a barbed-wire fence. Those barbs are sharp. Her aunt had been an Olympic high jumper, so Sherry had to uphold the family tradition. There was, however, one area where I could beat her: the hundred-yard dash, which we would run at the beach. It bugged her that she couldn't beat the old champ, no matter how much she clenched her teeth and strained.

Guns fascinated her, so we would, on occasion, do a bit of target shooting. Once I took Sherry pheasant hunting on a game farm in New Jersey. She loved it, but in her enthusiasm, she took a shot she shouldn't have and sprinkled bird shot on the roof of a house. Yipe! Either the occupants were not at home or hard of hearing. No one came out.

One beautiful spring day, Sherry seemed depressed. I asked, "What's the matter?"

She replied, "Art school will be over pretty soon, and my folks are insisting that I come back to Winnipeg. I'd rather stay here with you."

"I want you to stay here with me forever."

"Do you love me"

"Yes, I love you."

"I know I shouldn't ask this, but could we get married? Then I could stay with you forever."

"But Sherry, I don't want to go to a justice of the peace. It's too much like taking out another license. And I don't really want to have a wedding where you invite people—it gets too involved. You know what I'd like to do? I'd like to elope. You know, escape to some far-off island. I want something romantic. I understand the island of Bermuda is a delightful place."

Sherry's eyes lit up and she gave a super smile. "Yes, I'd love that."

"I'll talk to Frank Dodge, my producer, about getting a week off the soap. I'm not running very heavy right now." (Pause) "Sherry, what have we done?"

She said, "Kiss me long and hard so I don't cry."

I followed her advice, and she let out a war whoop—not ladylike, but heartfelt. I said, "Hey, Sherry, we're engaged."

Investigation turned up some pertinent information. We would have to establish residence for a few days in Bermuda prior to getting married. So why not have our honeymoon first, then get married? Definitely a cart before the horse operation, but what the hell. Life for most of us is an endless series of adjustments. I got on the phone and made our reservations.

Bermuda turned out to be a beautiful semitropical island. On our trip to the hotel, a horse-drawn carriage trotted us by pastel homes, with pristine white roofs that catch rainwater for drinking. The beaches of white sand are heavenly, and the sea is powder blue. We could hardly wait to plunge into that beautiful water. We had no problem placing the honeymoon ahead of the marriage.

Our marriage took place in Hamilton, Bermuda. It felt romantic and special. Then next day, we hopped a plane back to New York so I could continue my "Search for Tomorrow." I'd rather have searched for, and found, a few more idyllic days in Bermuda, but life can't be all wine and roses.

27

Artists at Work—and Play

ithin the great metropolis of New York City, there flourishes a
unique village, complete unto itself in its structure and appearance.
It is Greenwich Village. It has its own newspaper, *The Village
Voice*. Its streets are more happenstance and angular than Manhattan's
orderly grid, its natives more artistic and Bohemian than their wealth-ori-
ented neighbors to the north and those Wall Street gamblers to the south.

I had for years harbored a secret yen to live in Greenwich Village. The
lifestyle was casual: older Italian men playing bocce ball, a butcher shop
on Bleecker Street with white rabbits hanging in the window, coffee shops,
art exhibits, and MacDougal Street. What a wonderful name for a quaint
street—so Irish. Could be Scotch. If it were, I'd drink it, because I'm Irish.
However it was impractical to even think about the Village when Jan and
I had a beautiful apartment in midtown Manhattan—under rent control.

But now the cards had been shuffled and redealt. In my new life with
an artist wife, Greenwich Village was the only place to be.

Our one-bedroom apartment on the fourth floor was rather conven-
tional except for a terrace, which overlooked backyards. This gave our
apartment a whole new dimension. We had a barbecue grill on our terrace,
and it afforded us a bird's eye view of tree tops and assorted greenery—an
oasis in the cement jungle of Manhattan.

The apartment building was located on the perimeter of "Little Italy,"
where the bakery baked Italian bread twice a day to insure freshness,
where the owner of the neighborhood liquor store greeted me with "*bona
sera*," where mass was recited in Italian in an ancient Catholic church. In
the summer months, hucksters invaded our neighborhood with horse-

drawn wagons loaded with fresh fruits and vegetables, announcing their presence with shouts and a bell.

One Saturday morning, Sherry took brush in hand and started to paint and I took script in hand and started to memorize. All was as it should be. The artists creating in their chosen fields. This blissful quiet was sustained for fifteen or twenty minutes. Then Sherry, in a frenzy of frustration, threw down her brush and palette. A temper tantrum of fair magnitude erupted. Not quite frothing at the mouth, but near to it, she shrieked "Shit!" Her temper tantrums and moods of artistic frustration were of a scope and intensity that would fit nicely into a Greek tragedy like *Medea.*

I, as elder statesman and man of the house, felt that I should be of some help at a time like this, so I came up with "Sherry, maybe you should try modeling for a change."

Normally, such a stupid suggestion would only fan the flames of her rage, but she astonished me by shifting her mood gears and saying, "Maybe I should!"

"Okay," said I. "Monday, I'll set up an appointment with a photographer to have some pictures made, and we'll take it from there."

After a few minutes, she returned to her painting and I to my memorizing. I stole a glance. She really was a classic picture of that little girl who had a little curl right in the middle of her forehead: when she was good, she was very, very good, but when she was bad, she was horrid. Why was she that way? Was it her beautiful red hair that gave her such a flamboyant temper? Back to your lines, actor, yours is not to reason why, yours is but to learn the lines and make them sing as though you just thought of them.

On Monday I called a friend who gave me the name of a photographer. The shoot was scheduled for that coming Friday.

I had a rough week "Searching for Tomorrow." A couple of times I thought I'd found it. I made it through Friday, so I deserved a reward. On the way home, I picked up the ingredients from which lovely martinis are made, Tanqueray Gin, dry vermouth, and two lovely yellow lemons. Living dangerously, yes, but you only go around the track once. Sherry and I were in the mood for a bit of celebrating.

I toasted, "Here's to love and unity, dark corners, and opportunity."

We clinked our glasses.

"So how was the shoot?" asked I.

"Fine."

"When will he have the proofs?"

"Next Wednesday."

She didn't seem inclined to elaborate, so I got off the subject. I swear I seek peace in this world. I don't often find it, but I do seek it.

After two or three martinis, we wandered up Sixth Avenue, crossed Houston Street, and went to Leone's, an Italian restaurant with good food, red wine, and a walled-in back yard. Sometimes the neighborhood cats would use the top of the wall as a walkway when they headed out for their nightly prowls. If we were lucky, we might even see "Growltiger," a really tough looking feline.

Dinner was delightful. When we got back to the apartment, we were feeling no pain.

"You haven't said much about your session with the photographer, Sherry. Was it good? Was it bad? What?"

She hesitated, then, "Well, at the end of the session he asked me if I'd mind taking a topless shot; he had a topless job coming up."

"You posed topless? I suppose if he'd asked you to pose nude, you'd have eagerly kicked off your panties? Son of a bitch, I can't believe it."

So, like the racehorses at Belmont Park, we were off and running. A heated argument raged back and forth. Then she came in with a climactic question: "You don't love me, do you?"

"At this moment, I sure as hell don't."

That seemed to put a capper on the argument, so I sat down and started to read the paper. After a few moments, Sherry moved swiftly from the closet to the bathroom. As she was closing the door, I saw she was carrying my shotgun in its case. She slammed the door and locked it.

I should have beat on the door and begged her to come out and pleaded with her not to kill herself, but after a week of acting on a soap opera, I really didn't feel up to another hysterical scene, so I played it cool. However, when the gun went off, I lost all that cool. Did I ever! By now I knew that Sherry was capable of bizarre behavior. How bizarre? That I didn't know.

So I pleaded with her. "Sherry, darling, please say something. Sherry, what have you done? Sherry?"

Finally she said, "I'm all right." And she opened the door. The game of one-upmanship was over. She marched out, victorious.

I walked into the bathroom cautiously. My 1897 Winchester pump gun was lying quietly on its side in the bathtub. A 12-gauge shotgun at close range is a devastating weapon. It can take the head right off a rabbit. My trusty weapon had shot a hole in the bathtub, about an inch in diameter. The shot went right through the cast iron of that bathtub. The hole was located near the bottom, under the handles.

Surely someone must have heard that explosion. I kept waiting for a knock at our front door and the inevitable question, "What the hell's going on in there?" My mind was racing, but I kept coming up with dumb answers like, "Don't worry, officer, we were just shooting fish in the bathtub. Surely you've heard of shooting fish in a barrel, well, we were just ..." At this point the handcuffs would click shut as they encircled my wrists.

Seriously, what was I going to say if a the knock came? How about— "We heard that noise too, officer, but we thought it was a truck, out on Sixth Avenue, backfiring."

The knock never came. Then I remembered it was Friday. Thank God it was Friday night. Our close neighbors must be out on the town. But what in the name of God am I going to do about a one-inch hole in the bathtub? If I report it, question number one will be, "How did it happen?" Answer, "Well, I was fooling around with my electric drill and it jumped out of my hand and before I could catch it, it drilled a hole in the bathtub. Crazy little machine."

The tub would have to be replaced. But that's got to cost a bundle. Maybe I could fix it. The hole is close to round. I could take a rat-tail file and make a perfect round, then drive a cork into the hole. There's a slight bevel where the force of the shot bent the metal of the tub in. I could plaster over the cork and get a smooth surface. I found a few chips of paint which I carefully placed in a piece of tissue. I could have a paint shop duplicate the color. Worth a try. Anything other than going to the superintendent of the building and saying, "Have you got a minute, Jim? I want to show you something."

Now I knew what I'd be doing tomorrow.

Sherry had gone back to painting. The long-stemmed rose really has some thorns. Big ones. Guess we'd better make up. Maybe she'd like to play house. I surely didn't want to play another game of one-upsmanship with her. Not tonight, anyway.

Next morning I headed for the hardware store. My strategy for repairing the hole in the bathtub worked rather well. When I finished, it was barely noticeable. The paint match was not perfect. It looked as though a spot of paint might have fallen from the ceiling when it was last painted.

One night when I was relaxing in a hot tub of water, I projected far into the future when some luckless tenant lolling in a hot tub of water— much as I—would thrust his big toe into my repair job. The cork would have lost its stopper ability due to age and would collapse under the pressure of his big toe, allowing the contents of the tub to flow freely out and down. Where? I'd rather not think about that.

28

Go West, Young Man

*E*ach year the writers and the producer of "Search For Tomorrow" would meet for a story conference to discuss the upcoming year's story line. I can only compare this to the Greek gods meeting on Mount Olympus to decide the fate of poor mortals on earth. The big question that year was "What should we do with Arthur Tate? He's a reformed alcoholic, a has-been philanderer, a minion of his rich Aunt Cornelia, and he's had two heart attacks. What if we gave him a third and final seizure? Joanne could weep buckets of tears, suffer as only Joanne is capable of suffering, then recover and find a new love."

The gods had spoken. When I heard that Arthur was going to have a third and final coronary, I determined that I would give our viewers a heart attack they would never forget. I had seen the movie *Ship of Fools* where Oscar Werner had a fabulous heart attack up on the deck at night. I had envisioned Arthur Tate in the throes of a massive coronary, staggering under the weight of untold agonies. Then just before I collapsed on the floor, I would cry out "Joanne!" Joanne would enter the room, see me lying there and say, "Arthur," faintly, with terror in her voice. No answer. Then she would let out a blood-curdling scream. The camera would cut to Arthur lying on the floor, very still. Then the picture would fade as the organ crescendoed ominously. That would be our Friday curtain. In soap opera parlance, "a cliff-hanger." Housewives would be phoning each other all weekend, asking the big question, "Do you think Arthur Tate is really dead?" Dental appointments would be cancelled for Monday, because no self-respecting soap opera fan would dream of missing Monday's show.

When the script for my death scene arrived, I couldn't believe what our writers had written: "Arthur is driving his station wagon down the highway. He feels a pain in his chest, pulls over on the shoulder. Cut to a highway patrolman in a phone booth, telling Joanne her husband is dead." My death scene, which I had envisioned as the climax of a Greek tragedy, was phoned in by a highway patrolman.

I didn't mind leaving the show after twelve years, but I really hated the prosaic manner in which I expired.

Having found "Tomorrow" in the make-believe world, I now had to deal with tomorrow in the real world. It was not likely that I would be hired by another soap opera in the near future because I was too identified with "Search For Tomorrow." It would take some time to erase the Arthur Tate image, so Sherry and I decided to head for Hollywood. She had never been to California and always wanted to go there, and I wanted to see if I couldn't pick up some movie work in Hollywood.

One gray, January day, we zoomed through the Holland Tunnel in our cream-colored T-Bird and headed west. What a glorious feeling of freedom to be out of crowded New York and to be unshackled from that dreary soap opera where laughter was seldom heard. A new and better life was waiting for us in the west. By late afternoon we had reached the middle of Pennsylvania. All of a sudden, snowflakes began to fill the air. We turned on the car radio. Weather forecasters were excitedly talking about a winter storm. Then one weather person suggested that we might be in for a blizzard. Sherry gave a big cheer. What did she care? She had grown up in Winnipeg, Canada, where blizzards were a part of winter.

I said, "We'd better find a motel with a pool and a bar. We could get snowbound."

Sherry responded with "I'd love it."

We found a motel with all of the amenities: pool, sauna, restaurant, and bar.

I said, "Let's celebrate. Let the blizzard blow. We're safe here, and this is the end of an era and the beginning of a new life."

So we celebrated. Big time. While the blizzard blew.

The next morning was a bit headachy. I wrote a poem despite my headache, or perhaps because of it:

Hangovers, A Pair

Darling, whisper; don't move; let me kiss you.
The three-inch journey to your sleepy lips
Must be accomplished in languid fashion,

Like the slow drift of white clouds.
Ever so lightly will I kiss you,
As though the shadow of my lips had fallen on yours.

Then by a kiss will we unite two throbbing pains
And let our hangovers meet each other;
Twin headaches in therapeutic bliss.

Next morning we headed west through a beautiful world of dazzling white. A few vehicles were still stuck in snowdrifts. One monster truck lay quietly on its side.

We stopped for a couple of days in Kansas City to visit the relatives: my sister Kathleen and her husband, Joe, and their sons, Joe and Craig, and my darling mother. Our first evening in K.C., we were taken to Mission Hills Country Club for dinner, and it reminded me of my high school days.

It was here at Mission Hills that I made my social debut. I had recently become a member of Kappa Alpha Phi fraternity, and this was my first dinner dance. I was truly a country bumpkin. I started to follow the girls into the ladies' room. I got through dinner without any mishaps, but on the dance floor, I was a disaster. I only knew one dance step, which I repeated over and over—stiffly, I might add. My dancing partners must have heaved enormous sighs of relief when someone would tag me and cut in. In time, I became quite adept at this sort of social function, but that first dinner dance was a lulu.

Our stay in Kansas City was delightful. The Kellys were perfect hosts, but there is a means of communication called body language, expressed in attitudes and glances. From this nonverbal language, I concluded that my family felt I had not chosen wisely when I wed the long-stemmed rose. My mother, bless her heart, did ask what I planned to do with my career. I tried to reassure her by saying that to be at liberty is part of every actor's life, and that I wasn't worried about my future. But I could see that she was.

With many good-byes and lots of good lucks, we left the Kellys, but before we headed west, I wanted to see 7411 Terrace, the house where I grew up. It was only a mile or so away. It was a Dutch Colonial my dad had designed and built. It had been well cared for. The big walnut tree still grew by the side porch. It brought back many pleasant memories. I looked at it for a moment, smiled at Sherry, and then we headed west.

The world through which we traveled was covered with snow. The Grand Canyon looked even more spectacular trimmed in white. We signed up to take a mule ride down into the canyon, but it snowed some more that night and the ride was cancelled. So again we headed west, knowing we would soon be out of winter's grip in sunny California.

29

Xmas Dropouts

EN YEARS HAVE SPUN themselves into space since that enchanting Christmas night in Sturbridge, Massachusetts. Another unforgettable Christmas is on the horizon.

There is no snow to brighten the night, for this is Hollywood, land of make believe. Instead of going to Leiderkranz Hall with my head crammed full of memorized lines, I stand impatiently in the unemployment line.

As I stand there with my peers, slowly inching forward toward the cashier, my mine is awhirl—my problem, how to drop out of Christmas? I mean whole hog: no presents, no cards, no shopping, no nothing. Zilch participation. But how? Go camping. Good! But where? The desert? But Christmas is pervasive—mountains, deserts—it's everywhere. What about Death Valley? Death Valley! I've always been fascinated by the name. The moon would, of course, be the ultimate place, but a trip to the moon would attract too much attention. "Sixty Minutes" would want to cover it. Mike Wallace would try to pry the lid off my brain with questions like, "What are you, some kind of misanthrope?" "What did Santa Claus ever do to you?" Andy Rooney would frost the cake with a homespun on "dropouts don't deserve unemployment checks." Forget the moon. Death Valley it is. I rushed home to tell Sherry of my plan.

I headed the T-Bird up the snaky Nichols Canyon road to my Mexican ranch house in the hills. I almost collided with a motorcyclist who was speeding down the mountain, riding the dividing line of the road on a blind turn. Why would he do that? Did he have a death wish or was he just another idiot on two wheels? Oh well, happily, I missed him.

Sherry loved my game plan. She jumped up and down and clapped her hands.

I said, "You know, Sherry, there aren't too many campers at this time of year and we are apt to find ourselves alone in a remote area. I think I should buy us a pistol for protection."

She agreed wholeheartedly. This was a wonderful moment of togetherness. A journey into the unknown to escape the known. We were unique. All the others were slaves to Santa Claus. We had neither commitment nor conflict. Sherry started assembling the camping gear and I went down to a gun store on Hollywood Boulevard and bought a Luger-type pistol.

The trip to Death Valley was uneventful but full of anticipation. What struck me first about Death Valley was its starkness. It's as if the earth had taken off its clothes and was standing there naked before your astonished eyes. Every gully, every escarpment revealed, in brilliant sunlight. Alluvial fans spread out on valley floors, a product of massive erosion that continues each time it rains—which is very seldom.

We consulted our map and chose Stove Pipe Wells, which was on the edge of sand dunes that stretched off into the distance like the Sahara Desert. Here, in a campground, we pitched our tent. The temperature, which has been known to reach an unbelievable 134 degrees in the summer, was quite pleasant in December.

After we got our tent put up, we decided to do some target practice with our new pistol, so we got a coffee can from the manager of the campground and started across the sand dunes. What a strange world this was. It seemed to roll on forever. I took my compass, for it occurred to me it would be easy to get lost in this treeless, trackless desert.

We shot all our shells at the coffee can, then like spoiled children looked for a new game to play. We didn't find a new game, we found an old game in a brand new setting: we made love in the sand dunes, in the brilliant sunlight of Death Valley. Alone in a treeless, plantless universe, as though we were the first couple on earth — or perhaps the last.

That evening, a camper truck moved into the campground. They pulled in rather close to our tent, considering the amount of space available. We were willing to adjust to this intrusion until they started playing Christmas Carols with the volume turned up high. We felt this constituted an invasion of our privacy. They were forcing us to listen to the very thing that we were trying to get away from. It was when Gene Autry started to sing "Rudolph the Red Nosed Reindeer had a Very Runny Nose" that the shit hit the fan. It ignited in Sherry, whatever it was that got ignited in her at stressful moments like this. She sprang to her feet and stalked out of the tent, stiff-legged and oozing rage and determination. She visited our Christmasy neighbors and pointed out that we couldn't move because we were staked to the earth. They, on the other hand, had wheels so would they please get those wheels moving. I wish I could have seen their faces when this tall, red-headed misanthrope delivered her message. The poor woman probably made an entry in her diary: "We met an Antichrist in Death Valley and got the hell out of there fast!"

I've no doubt that in the misty future, MLT will offer package trips to the moon, but I contend that a trip to Death Valley will always be the poor man's chance to explore some fantastic moonscapes. At its lowest point, Death Valley is 235 feet below sea level. But it also has high mountains that are denuded and eroded, providing scenes of of dramatic desolation. Then there's the Devil's Golf Course, flat as a pancake, but its surface is so unbelievably rough you can't find a place to put your foot down because of the pointed, rock-like salt crystals that stick up everywhere.

The Ubehebe Crater was not caused by a meteorite smashing into the earth, but by underground lava flowing into underground water. This chance meeting caused a massive explosion that blew a big hole in the earth's surface. The very name, Furnace Creek, is a reminder not to go to Death Valley in the summer. But if you do, take lots of water.

We saw the desolate Panamint Mountains and two wild burros off in the distance. Death Valley Scotty's Castle is more like a large hacienda: Mediterranean in its concept with red-tile roof, arches, and turrets. There are several different stories about how Scotty came by his castle, but I like the one that says he struck it rich. Anyone who had the courage to prospect in Death Valley with a pickaxe and a burro deserved a few nuggets of gold.

South of Stovepipe Wells is Devil's Cornfield. From a distance, it looks like a field of corn shocks, but each shock is actually a plant called Arrow Weed. Zabriski Point, barren and stark, treeless and sunbaked, is surprisingly colorful. Some violent upheaval must have occurred in the past, because the strata now are vertical instead of in tiers, as God intended. Different colored strata form a massive, modernistic picture.

Death Valley is a startling place to see and some of its desolate views are actually quite beautiful.

Amazingly, animals live in this stark, forbidding land. Burros, whose owners died, or threw down their picks and simply walked away from their dreams of gold. Coyotes: I didn't see any, but I heard their tenor voices in a predawn harmony that caused my spine to tingle. Jack Rabbits, with long ears and astonishing speed, disappearing into the sparse vegetation. Then a large assortment of the uglies: lizards, tarantulas, snakes. None of the above in abundance, but that anything exists through the long, hot summer of Death Valley bears testimony to the ability to adapt of all living things. The law of the desert: adapt or die.

If you are looking for a place to hide from Santa and his reindeer, try Death Valley—the ultimate retreat.

30

Ride 'Em, Cowboy

THE DEATH VALLEY EXPERIENCE rekindled my boyhood dreams of cowboys and Indians and the wide open spaces. I grew up believing that I was a cowboy and that when I became a man, I would say "adios" to my tearful family and gallop off into the sunset. I could see myself loping through the purple sage with dark mountains looming on the distant horizon and danger lurking up ahead.

Having a horse of my own made this cowboy dream almost a reality. I had cowboy boots and a cowboy hat that I always wore. I can still hear T. A. O'Sullivan carping, "God, I wish you'd take that cowboy hat off long enough to get a little sun on your face." He didn't realize that real cowboys almost never take their hats off and usually die with their boots on.

This cowboy fantasy started when we moved to the very edge of Kansas City. A few of the neighborhood kids had ponies that they staked out in vacant lots.

One day I asked my dad if I could have a pony. He said, "Sure, but first you have to earn half of the money to buy it."

Good old Timothy Aloysius taught his son, Terry, the basic work ethic: earn the money and you can have almost anything you want. So I caddied for my dad, who was an avid golfer, and mowed the neighbor's yard. I was ready, willing, and able to do any job if it paid.

Meantime, I watched the ads in the *Kansas City Star*—"Horses for Sale." One day I spotted an ad that caused my adrenaline to flow. "Horse, saddle, and bridle, sacrifice $20.00." I made an appointment and that evening my dad drove me out to Overland Park, Kansas.

On the way out, Dad said "Offer them $17.50."

"Why?"

"Because" said he, "that's how horse trading is done. Just try it. The ad sounds like they're eager to sell."

Sure enough, they accepted my offer, so I came up with $8.75. My dad counted out $8.75. At the age of nine I became the proud owner of a horse named Sport.

He was a bay, reddish-brown, with a black mane and tail and a Roman nose. Not a very handsome fellow, but what could you expect for $17.50? Sport had a mean streak in him a mile wide. When the weather turned cold, watch out for those back feet. Ever hear that old expression, "He's got a kick like a mule"? I don't know what a mule's kick is like, but I sure know the feeling of Sport's hind hoof—it's like being hit with a baseball bat. I caught that hind hoof on my upper left arm and—oweee! I gave those hind feet a wide berth after that.

Then when I tightened up the saddle girth, he might turn his head and nip at me. Another charming habit Sport had was a proclivity for bathing. He loved to take baths. If you were crossing a small stream and allowed him to put his head down for a drink, it was only a matter of seconds until he would kneel down, then roll over in the water. Guess what happened to you? Hopefully it was a warm summer day. I began to understand why those Overland Park people were willing to sacrifice dear old Sport for $17.50.

Once when Charlie Hopkins and I were riding our steeds, we met up with two other kids on ponies. We rode along together, then these kids wanted to trade mounts for a ride. This we gladly did. We had gone only a short distance when we came to a mud hole. I winked at Charlie Hopkins and said, "Shall we let the horses have a drink?" Good old Sport took one gulp of water, then down he went with a very surprised and soon-to-be muddy and dripping rider. Guess Sport wasn't the only one in that group with a mean streak. Ah, yes, boys will be boys.

Spring rains softened the earth, and Sport pulled up the wooden stake that tethered him to the vacant lot where he grazed. Despite the fact that he had a twenty-foot chain attached to his halter, I had the damnedest time catching him. The thing that drove me mad was his attitude when he was loose. He would hold both head and tail up high like those high-stepping Hackney horses at the American Royal Livestock Show. He seemed to enjoy this chase, which I hated. Dusk was upon us as Sport cut through the Johnson's back yard. I was really moving it and Sport's chain was almost within reach. In the gathering shadows, I failed to see a wire clothesline that caught me right under the chin. My feet kept going but my head stayed. I leveled out in mid-air, then dropped to earth with a thud that knocked the wind out of me. As I lay there gasping for breath, I said, "That does it, Sport, you smart-ass. I'm trading you in."

I put an ad in the paper: "Horse, saddle, and bridle. Will sacrifice $27.50." I figured that price would give me some leeway for horse trading. Sure enough, a man offered me $25.00. I didn't jump at the offer. I suffered a little with "should I or shouldn't I," then accepted. I wanted to tell him "Watch those back feet, Mister, and for God's sake, don't let him take a drink if you're crossing a stream." But like an old horse trader, I clammed up and said, "Good-bye, Sport. It's been fun knowing you," and gave him a pat on his Roman nose, hoping he wouldn't snap at me. Thus ended an association which lasted about a year.

Now I was in the bucks. Twenty-five dollars for Sport plus $15.00 in the bank. I wanted to buy a real cow pony. It took some time, but I finally found what I was looking for—a Western cow pony named

Why didn't they tell me to sit down?
1927

Dolly. She was black with a white-blazed face and a glass eye. Not literally glass, but a white eye, sometimes called an agate eye—the mark of a true Western pony.

Horses are like people. There are winners and there are losers. Dolly was a winner: good disposition and really fast, she could turn on a dime and give you a nickel change.

This was the era of Tom Mix and Ken Maynard, cowboy movie stars. My favorite was Ken Maynard. He was a trick rider. When bullets started to fly, he would swing to the side of his horse. It looked as though his horse were riderless as it galloped by.

I watched his movies closely and imitated some of his tricks—like picking my hat up off the ground as I galloped past it. I learned to ride standing on the back of the saddle, walk, trot, canter. Then my big trick, which called for some coordination between horse and rider: I would stand on the left side of Dolly, reins in my left hand, both hands holding the horn of the saddle. Then I would say "Gitup!" As she started to move, I would pull myself up, knees bent, then as she broke into a gallop, I would drop my feet down, they would hit the earth, and the impact would throw me up into the saddle. Dolly and I put in some good years together.

By the time I was fifteen, the cowboy fantasy began to crumble. It would be a quick cop-out to say I discovered girls when I was fifteen. I discovered "a" girl when I was six years old and in the first grade at Bancroft School. Her name was Marcia Horst. She had long blonde hair, blue eyes, and a pretty smile. We used to walk home from school together. We might have been attracted to each other till the end of time, but in the second grade Marcia's family moved out of the neighborhood and she had to go with them.

For some, the boy/girl thing starts early and stays late. High school brought about big changes. I was invited to join a high school fraternity, Kappa Alpha Pi. This opened up a social whirl of Christmas parties, spring dances, and dates. Then when I was sixteen, I bought a Model-T Ford Roadster. It was "empty saddles in the old corral." My cowboy world crumbled and I became a part of the twentieth century.

I outgrew my dream of being a cowboy, but I never outgrew my love of horses. They are magnificent creatures. A special bond can develop between a man and his steed. Sometimes it seemed to me that we became one. My horse's power became my power as we raced across the prairie, with the wind in my face and the pounding of hoofbeats in my ears, and in my hand was the strength to control this powerhouse of motion that I was astride.

Some people bond to their cars in a similar fashion. I understand that, but I could never achieve with a car the wonderful exhilaration I felt on a horse, racing down the road to anywhere. It was a feeling of unadulterated freedom. Some cowboy summed it up when he let out a loud, long "Yahooo!"

31

Pistol Packin' Mama

You stand statuesquely on the shore,
The sea wind tossing your red, gold hair;
I call, "Sherry", but the surf steals your name:
I swim frantically, the riptide is my rudder;
I am drowning with your image in my eyes.

Sherry and I had some ties that bound us together: joie de vivre, outdoor activity, and strong physical attraction. One thing we did not have going for us was alcohol. When we drank, we tended to get into trouble.

During this California sojourn, I was mostly unemployed. I picked up a run on "Days of Our Lives," I did a few commercials, but the unemployment office was the planet around which I gravitated.

In retrospect, I should have found a job. But I didn't. We should have gone to a marriage counselor, but I didn't want to. Following one of our bouts, I moved out, stating, "I have but one life to live, and I sure as hell don't want to live it like this."

Meantime, Sherry took a job at a real estate company that auctioned off properties. We were separated, but not completely separated. We couldn't seem to live together or apart, so we lived somewhere between. One day Sherry asked if she might have the pistol, since she was living alone and it was scary up there in the hills, so I gave it to her.

Sherry's real estate company had scheduled a big auction in Palm Springs. She asked me if I'd like to join her on the Palm Springs expedition. I replied, "Yeah. Sounds like fun." So we drove out to the desert resort in her rented convertible. This was one of our togetherness moments when life seemed beautiful. The real estate auctioneers put on a big cock-tail party to publicize their upcoming sale. Sherry and I attended the party, sipping cocktails, smiling and chatting. Then we decided to visit Don the Beachcomber's for dinner. We dined on rumaki and shrimp, washed down with fruit juice that was heavily laced with rum.

When we said "aloha" to Don, we were more than mellow. I was the designated driver. I handed the parking attendant a tip. He said nothing. So I asked, "Can't you say 'thank you'?" And he dutifully said "Thank you."

As we drove off, Sherry turned on me with fury because I had been such a smart-ass with the parking attendant. You'd have thought I called her mother a whore. The lovers sped down the quiet streets of Palm Springs, hurling invectives at each other.

I stopped at a stop sign, Sherry reached over, turned the motor off and removed the keys with one swift movement. Then she ordered me to get out.

I replied, "Get out? What the hell are you talking about? I don't have a car."

Then she opened her purse, took out the pistol, and pointed it at my midriff, repeating her command, "Get out!"

My actor self asked, "What would 007 do at a time like this?" My cowardly self replied, "To hell with 007. Smooth talk the lady; get out of this car alive. Move slowly."

This I did and the pavement felt remarkably soft and friendly under my feet.

Then she pointed her pistol at the star-studded sky and pulled the trigger. It went off, shattering the night's silence. I stood there, transfixed, as she sped off into the darkness.

"Oh, my God," thought I, "that gun was loaded and probably off safety when it was aimed at my liver. Move it, man. Get the hell out of here. Now!"

I remembered that we had passed a filling station a couple of blocks back, so I headed in that direction, on the double. With the help of my plastic, I was able to have a rental car delivered to the filling station. Then I headed it west, toward L.A.

As I drove through the night, I thought, "Terry, you've had your warn-ing. If you go back to this crazy lady and get yourself killed, it will be your own fault. Get out of this mess, for Christ's sake. Go back to New York. Hollywood isn't your town."

A few days after the shootout at Palm Springs, I had a meeting with a lawyer. I told him I had gotten a Mexican divorce from Jan Miner. Then later, after I married Sherry, New York State had declared Mexican divorces invalid.

The lawyer said, "It sounds to me like we might be able to get an annulment."

I replied, "That would be heaven, since annulments don't pay alimony and I'm unemployed."

The lawyer was correct and we were able to get an annulment. Then I grabbed a plane for New York, grateful to be out of Hollywood and grateful to be single again.

Dear Red Dragon

Dear Red Dragon breathing fire,
Breathing hatred, resentment, ire,
Swear I love you! Swear I do!
Love! Love! Love! Love! Only you!

Dear Red Dragon, breathing flame;
Believe me, you are not to blame;
Satan built a fire in you,
Just to make you sweet to woo.

Dear Red Dragon, seething smoke,
If only I could, your fires, stoke,
'Til the flames consumed you quite,
In the silence of the night:
Swear I love you! Swear I do!
Love! Love! Love! Love! Only you!

32
Retreat to N.Y.C.

When I reached Kennedy Airport, I phoned Billie's Registry, a telephone service, to reinstate myself as a customer and ask if I might use this address for my mail until I could find an apartment. Billie came on the line, delighted to hear that I had returned.

She said, "This is where you belong, Terry. You've always done well here. It will be good to have you back." Her words gave me a lift. New York had been good to me in the past; why not now?

There were old friends to contact, favorite restaurants to revisit. I decided to have my first dinner at Sardi's. Vincent was there and he really gave me a warm welcome. It felt good to be back in noisy, exciting New York City.

A few days later, I dropped by Billie's Registry to pick up my mail. A young lady by the name of Jill Melody was on duty. What a cute girl she was, and so friendly. As I left Billie's, I admonished myself, "No, Terry, she's too young. Concentrate on your career."

There were lots of contacts to renew. It felt stimulating to be in New York, phoning and making appointments. In Hollywood you were dependent upon your agent. They didn't want you to run around making business contacts on your own. New York had a different structure. Here I could work with several talent agents and contact as many ad agencies and production companies as I wanted. Since I was a pretty good salesman, New York was a better market for me. I didn't have to spend my days waiting for something to happen; I could get out and make it happen.

When I would check my phone service on Saturdays, I usually spoke to Jill. She was always talkative and very friendly. I hadn't, as yet, met anyone. It seems to me that attractive women are usually married or involved. You have to catch them at the end of a relationship. Meantime, I had found a studio apartment on East 56th Street, not far from the East River and not far from Billie's Registry. One day I asked Jill Melody if she'd like to come to my place for dinner. She accepted most graciously.

I still remember opening the door, and there stood a real, live Kewpie doll, petite and about as cute as they come. I said to myself, "Terry, if you screw up this seduction, you are going to commit hari-kari first thing tomorrow morning."

I'm ever so grateful that I did not have to terminate at this particular moment when a new chapter was just starting. When Jill awoke, she immediately smiled. No transition—she went from sleep to smile. Bingo. I can't tell you how that warmed my heart. The long-stemmed rose would likely have glared at me, then turned over. "New York, New York, it's a wonderful town, the Bronx is up and the Battery's down."

Jill Melody Gauron was an aspiring actress. She had attended the Neighborhood Playhouse and was now sending out photos with résumés attached, phoning and auditioning in a highly competitive world. That we had in common—the search for work.

One day, I got a call from Roy Winsor, producer of "The Secret Storm," a TV soap. Roy seemed to be studying me as we talked. Then he said, "Yes, I think you could play a judge. We're going to audition next week. I'll be in touch."

That was an audition I really needed to win because I was running out of chips. Whether it was my reading, my reputation, or Irish luck, I cannot say, but something fell into place and I became Judge Sam Stevens, a new character on "The Secret Storm."

In the cast of "Secret Storm" was Christina Crawford, Joan Crawford's daughter. She played the part of Joan Borman, a very difficult young lady, not at all like the Tina we actors knew and loved. The first day on "Secret Storm," Christina made a point of welcoming me aboard.

Not too long after I joined the show, Tina became ill and had to go to the hospital for an appendectomy. Someone in the production office had a truly brilliant thought: "What if we got Joan Crawford to play her daughter's part?" It was an offer Joan couldn't resist. Due to her Pepsi commitments, she could only tape on weekends. I cannot tell you the excitement Joan Crawford caused at the West 57th Street Studios of CBS.

From a dramatic point of view, it was preposterous. Joan and Tina were a generation apart. Tina was a blonde, Joan a brunette. They didn't resemble one another in any way, but from a showmanship point of view, it was utterly brilliant. The ratings of "Secret Storm" shot up. It made a

Judge Stevens of "The Secret Storm"

wonderful publicity story. "Joan Crawford covers for her daughter in a soap opera." All anybody at CBS could talk about was Joan Crawford, how she sipped vodka in her dressing room. Whatever Joan did, or didn't do, was whispered about in the corridors. It was like the second coming of Christ. Everyone was mesmerized by this former movie star.

I didn't play any scenes with Joan, but the scene that stands out in my memory was one she played with a lawyer, Mr. Fluellen. I don't remember the actor's name. The tape was rolling, Joan was slicing him up verbally, and then totally unrehearsed and unexpected, she backhanded him across the chest. He staggered back in wide-eyed horror. It was wonderful. I wanted to shout, "Hit him again, Joan." That was the take that our astonished viewers saw the following week on TV. Perhaps it was this kind of daring that made Joan Crawford a great movie star.

Then Tina returned, good as new, and "The Secret Storm" resumed its normal pace. But it seemed to me that Joan Crawford's ghost hung around CBS for several weeks.

I don't know just when it was that Jill moved in with me. It wasn't a move, really; it was a transition like drifting from spring into summer. One day you go fishing and the next thing you know, it's the Fourth of July. It worked rather well, actually. Jill could wash dishes, but she hadn't the faintest notion of how you dirty them. Cooking for me was a hobby and so betwixt the two of us, we lived quite nicely.

It's strange but if I don't have someone to cook for, I usually don't cook. Our dining area was a delight, up one step, bounded by a wrought iron fence on one side and windows on the other, attached to a small but efficient kitchen.

One day Jill came home with a pussy cat named Omar—the gift of a friend who was leaving town. Omar was jet black, trimmed with white. He had four white feet, a white dickey under his chin, and a wonderful white mustache. All this set off with bright yellow eyes that stared at you. He walked into our menage as though he owned the place, and before long, he did.

Life seemed rather idyllic at this point, but up in Brunswick, Maine, a storm was brewing. Jill's mother, Virginia, was most unhappy and fretful. Her only little baby girl was living in sin—with a man—an older man. No need to say how much older. Quite a bit older, actually. By phone and letter, Virginia launched a campaign against our little garden of Eden with its wrought iron fence and elegant pussy cat.

The solution to this growing problem seemed to be marriage. "Oh, dear, marriage? Let's see, that would be number five for me."

Jill was very close to her mother, so now there was thunder over paradise. Jill started saying, "Couldn't we, Terry? Mother is threatening to come down here." I felt myself beginning to weaken. I caught myself saying things like, "Oh, what the hell. One marriage more or less isn't going to hurt me, I suppose." A prospective bridegroom should have a more positive outlook when launching his craft onto the turbulent sea of matrimony, but I had been shipwrecked not once, not twice, not thrice, but four times. Yet I liked this funny little world I was living in and I was loathe to give it up. So I sat down and had a good talk with Omar. He begged me to summon up the courage to say "I do," so I did.

Jill was overjoyed. Her mother slept well for the first time in who knows how long. I even had a brilliant thought, "Let's get married in Puerto Rico. I love Puerto Rico and I've never been married there." So off we flew to San Juan.

The marriage ceremony was performed by a Puerto Rican lady judge. It was, to put it mildly, unique. It seemed to me that a bit of voodoo had found its way into the marriage ceremony, and I thought perhaps this mysticism is what was lacking in my other nuptial knot-tying ceremonies. Perhaps this will bind us together till death do us part.

To celebrate the tying of the knot, we went to a Puerto Rican restaurant where a whole pig is put on a spit in the window, and roasted. This roasted pork is served with fried plantains, and it really is delicious.

Next morning the O'Sullivans set out to explore El Morro fortress, which guards the entrance to the port of San Juan. What a massive stone structure it is. It occupies a point of land shaped like a spear, which thrusts out into the sea. The Spanish worked on it—not for generations, but for centuries—two centuries, in fact, from 1539 to 1787. This forbidding fortress turned back many a would-be invader. It wasn't until the Spanish American War in 1898 that the fortress fell and Puerto Rico became a territory of the United States.

Puerto Rico is an interesting mix of old and new. New modern hotels stand tall on its beautiful beaches, and Old San Juan with its Spanish colonial buildings reminds us that Christopher Columbus set foot on this island in 1493.

We really wanted to linger in this lovely tropical island but, alas, it was time to return to Manhattan, the island of cement, steel and reality.

33

Let's Go to Europe

One evening as I was opening the door to my apartment, thinking how good a Scotch and soda would taste, I was greeted by a smiling, bubbling Jill Melody. After a rather lengthy kiss, I asked, "What happened, did you win an audition?"

"No, Terry." Eye-to-eye contact for a moment, then out it came: "Let's go to Europe!"

"Europe? My God. That costs a fortune."

"No, it doesn't. I have some money in my savings account, and…"

"Wait a minute, Jill. Let me get a drink and sit down. Then tell me about it."

When I was properly seated, Jill began, eagerly, "Did I ever tell you about my friend, Camille?"

"No, I don't think so."

"Well, when I went to high school in Portsmouth, Maine, I took French, and one of our assignments was to trade letters with a student who lived in France. My teacher gave me the name and address of Camille Beauchene in Epernay, France. I would write Camille in French and she would respond to my letters in English. We became pen pals and this made the study of French much more fun, but we didn't stop writing when the school year ended. In fact, we've kept those letters going back and forth across the ocean for about six years now. I haven't heard from her for a long time, but this morning I got a letter from my mother, and in it was a letter from Camille. She wants to meet me, and says please come to France this summer."

"Hey, Jill, do you have any idea how much a round trip to France costs?"

"Yes, I bought a copy of the *Village Voice* today and Icelandic Airlines has this big ad in it with special rates to Europe."

So saying, she produced the *Village Voice*. In 1969, Icelandic was a cut-rate airline. Soldiers stationed in Europe and their wives used it almost exclusively. At that time, Icelandic still used propellers on their planes. All of the bigger airlines were jet propelled.

I was surprised. Their round trip tickets were much less than I thought they would be. I looked at Jill and said:

"Give me a day or two to think about it. A trip to Europe is a big project."

The more I thought about it, the more involved I became. I bought a book entitled *Europe on $5.00 a Day*. Although inflation had made the $5.00 a day passé, the book was full of practical ideas. For instance, if you can accept having your bathroom down the hall, you can save a bundle on hotel bills. Hotels in Europe were not constructed with a bath in every room. Eat the continental breakfast that comes with the room. Forget the bacon and eggs; that crusty French bread they serve is delicious. Pick up your lunch at a delicatessen. Then you eat only one expensive meal a day, your dinner. I bought a Berlitz French book so I could learn to *parle* a little *Français*. The upcoming trip gradually became the focal point of our lives. Jill wanted to meet her pen pal in Epernay, both of us wanted to spend a week in Paris, and I had a yen to visit a castle on the Rhine.

We left Kennedy Airport the morning of July 10 on Icelandic Airlines, our destination the Grand Duchy of Luxembourg, with a very brief stop in Reykjavik, Iceland. I was delighted that I would get to see Luxembourg. Grandmother Nesch's parents came from this tiny country. It's surprisingly small, about thirty miles across and fifty miles long. It is tightly wedged in between Belgium, France, and Germany. At one time, Luxembourg was known as the Gibraltar of Europe. Its hills are still filled with tunnels and ancient fortifications.

We picked up our European Ford at the Luxembourg Airport, and our adventure began. However, we were both showing symptoms of jet lag, so we checked into Hotel Cravat. As we were checking in, I turned to Jill and said, "Doesn't cravat mean tie in French?" She allowed as how it did, and started to laugh.

"Okay, Jill, you can laugh, but I'm learning to speak French, thanks to Monsieur Berlitz. You'll see, before this trip is over, I'll be speaking fractured French fluently."

Next day we headed south down through the wine country, stopping at several wineries to sample their wares. Ou la la, *bon*! Something wonderful happens when you become a tourist. It sharpens your senses. You look more closely, you anticipate, you compare, and if you are in the French wine country, you sample. *"Merci beaucoup, Monsieur."*

Late in the afternoon we reached Epernay, on the Marne River. Then with the help of Jill's high school French and the patience of a few French folk, we were able to locate the home of Camille Beauchene. As a French student, I was thrilled to recognize a familiar word here and there, but I wanted to say to these people, "Slow down, for Christ's sake." Alas, I didn't know how to say that in French, so I just listened and smiled.

We knocked on the door of the Beauchene home. The door opened, and we were greeted like long lost relatives. It was truly a privilege to be invited into the home of a French family. Camille had a younger sister, a teenager, Marie. Their father worked for the railroad. He was a friendly fellow, someone you liked from the first handshake. Her mother was all smiles and busy preparing dinner. Camille had invited her friend, Jeanne, to join us for dinner because she spoke good English. I was seated next to Jeanne at the dinner table, so she could help me follow the conversation.

The delicious dinner featured roast lamb, and there were fresh green peas from their garden. Jill and Camille were like long lost friends having a reunion. They actually knew a great deal about each other. This was an unforgettable moment in both their lives, and those of us in their presence felt the emotional impact of this very special meeting.

Next morning at breakfast, the laughter and conversation continued. Then Camille took us on a guided tour through a champagne winery. This was a unique experience because the winery was located in a huge cave. The proper aging of champagne must be done where the temperature is constant. The samples they graciously handed us were delicious and bubbly.

Finally, I said, "Ladies, I hate to be a party pooper but it's time for us to head for Paris."

The parting was sprinkled with tears, hugs, and laughter. Camille promised to visit us in New York. Then we said *au revoir* and headed west toward Paris.

Our first objective was to find La Riv Gauche, the left bank, for that was where the less expensive hotels were located. La Riv Gauche reminded me of Greenwich Village, so I immediately felt at home. We checked into La Porte Hotel, $9.00 a night, with bath down the hall and continental breakfast included. *Quelle difference?* We would be spending minimal time in our funky French hotel. Outside was a fascinating city waiting to be discovered.

When I was seven years old, our neighbor, Mrs. Davis, took me to see *The Hunchback of Notre Dame* starring Lon Chaney. That picture stamped itself in my memory with indelible ink. I can still see his ugly face and deformed body crawling like a spider around the stone gargoyles of Notre Dame. Then when he rang those huge church bells by pulling ropes, the bells would lift him up in the air as they tolled. When the peasants revolted and were storming Notre Dame, the hunchback, with superhuman strength, picked up a huge beam and hurled it down on the crowd, pinning half a dozen of them to the earth, their arms and legs waving helplessly in the air.

Notre Dame had to be our first stop in Paris. *Voila*! It was only a few blocks from our hotel. The Cathedral of Notre Dame stands elegantly in the Seine River on an island. It seemed much more sedate and dignified than in those turbulent times when Quasimodo was the resident bell ringer. We ventured inside the cathedral and there was such an aura of beauty and peace, that I knelt down, crossed myself, and said a few prayers. Then I gave thanks that I was privileged to come here and meet "Our Lady" in person.

When we stepped outside, the sun was shining and the river was sparkling. As we strolled along its banks, there were artists dipping their brushes and staring intently at their canvases. There were lovers strolling arm in arm. There were long river boats hauling their cargo up and down the Seine. This was the Paris we had dreamed about.

Excitement was pulsating through the streets of Paris. Tomorrow would be Bastille Day. On July 14, the French celebrate the fall of the Bastille and the start of the French Revolution. Our host at Hotel LaPorte told us that the Bastille Day parade would be *très magnifique*, and it truly was. Replete with bands, proudly marching soldiers, rumbling tanks, planes roaring overhead, and tricolor flags flying everywhere. For me, the most exciting moment was when the cavalry went prancing by. The mounted soldiers wore metal helmets with black plumes that responded to the gait of their beautiful horses.

That night, there were fireworks exploding around us, much like our Fourth of July celebration. Ever since that 14th of July, I remember Bastille Day by going to a French restaurant, or by giving a toast, or by just quietly remembering.

We sipped wine at a sidewalk cafe on Champs-Élysées, watching humanity stroll by and commenting on same, as though we were judges placed on this earth to sort out and categorize humanity. We ascended the Eiffel Tower in tourist fashion, all agog and excited by our birds-eye view of Paris. We came, we saw, we were conquered. I strongly suspect that I'm a Francophile, or that I could easily become one with a nudge and a glass of *vin rouge*.

I had a dream to fulfill. I wanted to visit an old castle on the Rhine, surrounded by forested hills and strategically placed on the heights above the river.

One morning while having our continental breakfast courtesy of Hotel LaPorte, Jill and I got into a conversation with a German couple from Nuremberg. Their name was Schultz, and they spoke quite good English. When I told them of my desire to see a castle, they looked at each other and smiled. Then they told us about the beautiful castle in Heidelberg. That immediately caught my interest because I remembered that Heidelberg was the setting for a delightful operetta, *The Student Prince* by Sigmund Romberg.

The Eiffel Tower

Mr. Schultz hastened to add, "But Heidelberg isn't on the Rhine. However, it's on the Nechar River."

Then Mrs. Schultz chimed in, "The city of Heidelberg is so quaint and charming, you'll fall in love with it."

We promised our new friends that we would visit Heidelberg and thanked them profusely for their suggestion. Then we rushed upstairs to consult our maps. The trip to Heidelberg would cause no major changes in our itinerary. We had planned to drive straight east of Paris to Strasburg, which is on the Rhine River. At this point, the Rhine forms the boundary line between Germany and France. About seventy miles north-northeast is Heidelberg, situated on the Nechar River, near where it joins the Rhine.

When we reached Strasburg, we took a boat trip on the Rhine, but it was much like taking that boat trip around Manhattan Island—everything was big town and highly industrialized, so we cut short our stay and headed north to Heidelberg.

The stone-arched bridge that spans the Nechar River is a perfect introduction to Heidelberg's old town. At the far side of the bridge stands a formidable stone gate framed by two tall towers, so ornate it's hard to believe their purpose was to guard. The old town, which lies beyond the gate, is enchanting. I found myself comparing it to illustrations in the book of Grimm's fairy tales.

We wandered down cobblestone streets, admiring the quaint houses and shops, then stopped in front of a restaurant with large, exposed beams in its stucco walls and a sign that said "Brahaus."

We looked at each other, and I said, "Shall we? It's lunch time."

Jill said, "Yes, I'm starved."

The Brahaus was at the peak of a busy lunch hour. Hearty German waitresses in white aprons were swinging through the crowded tables delivering mugs of beer and plates piled high with steaming food. We felt a bit overwhelmed but eager to join the festivities. Our host seated us at a table for two and we automatically ordered beer. Then we set about studying the menu. Jill chose wienerschnitzel. She admitted later that she had hoped the wiener might be a hot dog. It was veal. I knew that hasenpfeffer was rabbit in some form. The sound of the word fascinated me, so that was my choice.

As I continued to read the menu, it seemed to me that the Germans were excessive in their use of consonants and vowels. For instance the dish, schweinebraten, contains fourteen letters. We Americans call it roast pork, using only nine letters. Not a complaint, just a stupid tourist observation. Our entrees arrived surrounded by spaetzel and cabbage. The food was very tasty and the portions were generous. By the time we finished our lunch, I understood why our waitress seemed a tad overweight. It would be quite easy to increase one's avoirdupois with good German food like this, enhanced by mugs of zesty beer.

Thus fortified, we were now ready to explore the castle. The road leading up to the castle circled round and round the steep hill, so the ascent was gradual. We rounded the final curve and there it stood, the wondrous castle of Heidelberg. The reddish brown stone used in its construction gave it a special aura. The site was well chosen. It provided a commanding view of the Nechar River and the surrounding countryside.

In 1689, the castle had fallen to the French in a battle with Louis XIV. This siege left scars, but restoration efforts have brought parts of this mighty fortress back to its former glory.

In order to withstand a siege, castles had to be heavily provisioned with food and drink. In one of the storage rooms was an enormous barrel, surely the biggest barrel in the world. We were told that it had been a wine barrel.

Jill and I leaned on the ramparts of the castle watching a beautiful sunset fade into the west. At the precise moment when late afternoon becomes evening, the bells in the City of Heidelberg began to ring—not just a few, but a chorus of bells: sopranos, baritones, tenors, all ringing and reverberating in harmony, joyously announcing the end of another day. As we listened, I had a fantasy. The slumbering castle awakened and for a few moments lived again in all its splendor, peopled by knights and ladies. Then the bells stopped ringing and the illusion faded. But it was an unforgettable moment.

We turned for one last look at the enchanted castle. It had fallen asleep. Darkness had already crept into some of the vacant rooms. Time to say *auf wiedersehen*.

34

The Honeymoon Is Over

I WISH THAT I COULD WRITE those beautiful words, "And they lived happily ever after," but, alas, 'twas not to be. Kewpie doll was beginning
to pout. She no longer greeted the day with a smile—a trait which I
found most endearing. Her cuteness had turned to petulance. Jill's inability to get her career off the ground was the cause of her frustration. Now
she was beginning to blame me. She seemed to feel that I should be able
to extend my hand and take her right along with me, down the road to a
successful acting career.

I seemed unable to convince her that show biz doesn't really work
that way. Casting is not done from casting couches. Oh, yes, there are casting couches, but when the chips are down, everyone's job is at stake. Bad
casting can be costly.

I pointed out that "my contract on 'The Secret Storm' is coming up for
renewal. The way the story is running, I'm not at all sure that I will be
renewed."

She replied, "Oh, you'll get something. You always do. But what
about me?"

"Jill, I'm a performer. I don't have any jobs to hand out. Maybe you
should have married a producer."

Whoops, I shouldn't have said that. Now I needed to say something
positive.

"Look, why don't you get your friend Patty to come over and I'll
direct you two in some scenes."

That suggestion elicited a weak smile from Kewpie Doll, and she said,
"That would be cool."

My prediction was correct. "Secret Storm" did not renew my contract, and once again I found myself standing in line at the unemployment office. When I was in Hollywood, I became aware that many of the actors had other careers they pursued between picture assignments. I had resisted doing that in the past, but this time a little voice whispered "Don't wait too long, Terry. Do something now." I explored job possibilities and decided on real estate, because it seemed to adapt itself to an actor's life. When you get a show-biz job, you can turn your real estate client over to an associate. When you finish the acting job, you return to the real estate office and pick up where you left off.

I went to real estate school to learn about liens, escrows, and foreclosures. Not too exciting, but I usually managed to get a laugh out of each class without upsetting the teacher. Then came the state exam. I passed. Next move, get a job. So I made the rounds. Talman, Bigelow, and Whitimore hired me. They were located at 62nd and Madison. Most of my real estate activity had to do with leasing. Leases in New York City were written for two or three years. If the apartment rented for $1,000 a month, the contract could be for three years, or $36,000. A slice of that kept a salesman in business. Also I would pick up an occasional modeling job or a commercial. A year drifted by in this manner.

One morning I woke up and realized it was St. Patrick's Day, 1971, that day in March when the Irish march, disrupting the already slow flow of midtown traffic which then becomes hopelessly snarled. But the bands play, the marchers march, everyone wears something green, and it's a great day for the Irish.

I had an apartment showing that morning. When that was accomplished, I had a drink—or was it two—a toast to St. Patrick. Then I headed for the parade. Wouldn't dream of missing it. I caught up with it at 62nd and Fifth. High school bands, rag-tag Irish societies marching in and out of step. Then, all of a sudden, here they came, dressed in kilts and tams, marching smartly, playing bagpipes making that strange music that only bagpipes make. Something in my genes responded and I started to cry. Not a lone tear but several. I quickly put my glasses on and glanced around to see if anyone had discovered that I was shedding a tear or two. No one noticed. They, too, were enthralled by the wearing of the green and the skirl of the bagpipes.

When the marchers had passed, I ducked out and headed for a nearby bar. I wanted to evaluate this emotional upheaval I had just gone through. You see, I'm only half Irish. In my family we were not propagandized about how wonderful it is to be Irish. Actually, I was more aware of being

Catholic. How could I ever forget Catholicism, when each Sunday morning I was roused from my bed and urged on by Timothy Aloysius to hurry up and get dressed for Mass.

Anyhow, I was fascinated by my response to the Hibernian Marching Society and even considered joining some Irish club. Next day I sobered up and got over that urge, but I shall never forget that day those marching Irishmen with their bagpipes and kilts broke through my New York sophistication and touched a part of me that I didn't know I had.

My consumption of Scotch increased during this period. TV soaps do impose a discipline on an actor. Always there are lines to be learned, and alcohol definitely slows the learning process. Meantime, I worked with Jill on her acting. She and her girlfriend Patty would memorize scenes, and I would direct them. Jill was a pretty girl, a perfect ingénue type. She had lots of ambition, but she was a bit short on talent. That's tough when life gives you an enormous need to achieve but neglects to bestow on you the talent needed to achieve your goal. However, she did improve, and I found that I enjoyed the role of director.

One Friday evening, Jill, Patty, and I were working on a scene from *My Sister Eileen*. The rehearsal had gone well, so we celebrated by having a few drinks. With my directorial mind still in gear, I said, "Wouldn't it be fun if we all hopped into bed together?"

This suggestion caused much giggling and remarks like, "Really, Terry!"

"You've got to be kidding!"

Amid all the hubbub, I was unable to pick out any negative words. Next thing I knew, garments were floating floorward.

It really was a memorable evening. Just one of those things that happen because the time and place are right, or the moon is full, or the participants are half full, or all of the above.

It never happened again. It might have, but next day I received a phone call that changed everything.

35

The Old Log Theater

*T*HE PHONE CALL was from my good friend, Don Stolz of the Old Log
Theater in Minneapolis. Don said, "Terry, I apologize for giving
you such short notice, but rehearsal starts tomorrow and my leading man is in the hospital. Is it possible that you could come out?"

I replied, "Yes, yes, I can come. I have a modeling job at 9:00 A.M.
tomorrow. It will take an hour, two at the most. I'll check the plane sched-
ules and get right back to you. Thanks, Don."

My modeling job was for *True Confessions* magazine. I portrayed an
outraged father pointing an accusatory finger at his pregnant daughter.
Highly melodramatic. This is the kind of thing actors do when "at liberty"
but don't mention in their resumes.

When I told little Jill of my good fortune, she became pouty because
no one ever hired her. I said, "Hey, Jill, you and I are not competing with
each other—we're supposed to be—like, together." She was unable to
share in my good fortune. I promised her a trip to Minneapolis, but unhap-
piness clouded her pretty face as we said good-bye.

It was the last week of April, and as my plane took off, I felt like a wild
duck must feel when it heads back north in the spring. Free, flying through
the boundless sky, with a new adventure on the horizon. I felt reborn; out
of gray New York into beautiful Minnesota; out of escrows, closings, and
contingencies into a role that was right down my alley. The play was *Not
Now, Darling,* a British farce.

It's nice to have someone waiting for you at the end of your journey,
and there in that cluster of expectant faces was a smiling Don Stolz. It was
good to get back to Minnesota.

Seeing the Old Log Theater again was like coming home. It is located on the outskirts of the charming little town of Excelsior. It has a proscenium stage with a seating capacity of 655. An attractive restaurant, with an outer wall of windows, occupies another section of the building. In the lobby is a bar and a large stone fireplace where theater goers can warm their fingers on frosty nights. The wooden building is low, rustic, and blends in nicely with its rural surroundings. The Old Log is known as a comedy house, a place where people come to laugh.

Don had assembled a good cast for *Not Now, Darling*: Richard Weed, Ken Senn (a Zero Mostel look-alike), and Nancy Nelson, who looked utterly divine in panties and bra. This was a farce where scantily clad ladies were hidden in closets, when wives made unexpected visits. Ken Senn and I were business partners, a couple of furriers, he a square, I a swinger.

In the opening scene of the play, Ken was arranging mannequins in our showroom. He inadvertently grabbed a live model by the crotch to move her. She screamed, he blushed, the audience howled, and it went from there. A bit like *The Marx Brothers at the Circus.*

Also in our cast was a young actor named Nick Nolte. His behavior away from the theater was a bit flaky, but he took his acting seriously. I saw his script in the dressing room. He had carefully translated each of his speeches into his own words so his feeling and interpretation would be correct and sound believable.

There's a story about Nick Nolte his fellow actors like to tell, for it, like Nick, is rather unique. It's an actors' story that is usually told only in the dressing rooms or in bars. But for just this once, I'll tell the story to you.

The Old Log Theater was presenting *Harvey,* that delightful drama about a happy drunk, Elwood P. Dowd, and his companion, Harvey, a large white rabbit. Harvey is invisible, but when you sit in the audience, you know he is there. You can almost see him. Ken Senn was playing Elwood, Cleo Holladay the nurse, and Nick Nolte was Doctor Sanderson.

Remember, gentle readers, actors are human, they catch colds, have headaches, and all the other "natural shocks that flesh is heir to." They differ from other wage earners in this respect: no one can cover for them. In a theater like the Old Log, you do not have an understudy. Ergo, if you can walk, talk, and breathe, you perform. "The show must go on." I'm not sure why, but I know it must.

Nick Nolte was ill. He had the trots. I'd like to rephrase that—he had the runs. Were he in any other business he wouldn't dream of going to work, but he was in show biz. So at 8:00 P.M. he entered the dressing room

Example of a nuts and bolts modeling job:
Terry O'Sullivan and actor Ed Noreen in an
ad for Northwestern National Life Insurance Co.

looking like a sick ghost. His fellow actors admired his spunk but questioned his sanity.

The problem with acting is that when you get out on that stage and become involved in a scene, you are apt to forget your limitations and go for it. Nick went for it. He forgot that he was ill and what his illness was. Result: he had "an accident" on stage.

Shortly thereafter, the blocking of the play changed drastically. If Nick was stage left, the other actors managed to be stage right—far right. If Nick crossed right, they countered left. It looked as though they were trying to balance a sinking ship. Luckily, the curtain fell. No, *mercifully* the curtain fell.

Nick blamed it all on that damned white rabbit. Defensively, he shouted, "If Elwood can't house train that monster rabbit, he should leave him outside!"

It was noted that Nick had different trousers on for the second act.

Don Stolz remembers an industrial show he wrote and directed for Grain Belt beer. Nick Nolte was one of the actors who performed in the skits. After the show, the cast and some of the Grain Belt beer people went out for dinner. A waitress stopped at the table and inquired, "Can I get anyone something to drink?"

Right on cue, as if he were doing another skit, Nick spoke up, loud and clear, "Bring me a bottle of Bud." His unorthodox request stunned the celebrants into shocked silence. In that dreadful moment, Don Stolz saw the Grain Belt beer account float right down the Mississippi River.

The waitress, with pencil poised, said, "Is that it, then? One bottle of Budweiser?" Did she have to compound the felony by repeating that hateful word?

To this day, Don Stolz is not sure if Nick made this faux pas out of ignorance—as he professed—or out of derring-do, just to see what would happen.

Nick always lived close to the edge. People around him got into trouble, but he always came out smelling like a rose. He was a likeable fellow, on stage and off.

Now we return to the play, *Not Now, Darling,* which was in rehearsal. My part, Gilbert Bodley, was a large role, and I was hard put to learn all the lines and get them up to tempo in just eight days. The play was my constant companion. I ate with it, slept with it, talked to it.

Don has a talent when it comes to directing farce. He admonishes his actors, "Do not try to be funny. In a farce you are usually in trouble because you've told a lie. Now you must tell more lies to substantiate the first lie, and you get in deeper. Your need is to get out of this mess. This urgency gives the farce its tempo and reality."

I recall that during rehearsal we were all a bit worried about whether this crazy farce would finally come together and delight our audience. Then came opening night. The audience loved it. They laughed until they were tired of laughing. For an actor, there's nothing better than being in a hit show, whether it's on Broadway or in Excelsior, Minnesota.

Nick Nolte and Jimmie Wright shared a small house in Excelsior. They hosted the opening night party. Wow! What a party! Some time late in the evening, I had an enormous need for fresh air. I went outside and that wonderful, crisp air tasted so good, I decided to take a walk. Good idea, except that I got lost. I thought, "If I can locate Lake Minnetonka, I can follow around Excelsior Bay and get home." I found the lake and headed home, walking briskly. A night in early May can be quite chilly in Minnesota.

As I put my hand on the knob to open the door of my garage apartment, a nearby robin burst into song. Then, as though he had given a downbeat, every bird in every tree in the neighborhood joined in this pre-dawn symphony. I have been welcomed home, but never like this. Never with such joy. I thanked the beautiful birds for such an unforgettable welcome and went to bed.

My garage apartment was right on the lake. How wonderful to wake up on a spring morning, look out the window, and see sparkling Lake Minnetonka! This trip to Minnesota was truly a wonderful experience. In addition to a hit show and beautiful spring weather, there was fishing. Good fishing.

Minnesota is known as the land of ten thousand lakes, and every one of these lakes contains fish. Few people can resist the excitement that occurs when a frantic fish bends a fishing pole, then darts hither and yon, causing one's line to cut through the water and one's heartbeat to quicken.

When I was a boy, we made two trips to Minnesota, and this was when I got hooked on fishing. We vacationed at Little Pelican Lake in the vicinity of Gull Lake. Its water was remarkably clear and its shores were lined with beautiful pine trees.

The fishing expedition I remember most vividly was the day my dad took his three offspring fishing: myself and my two younger sisters, Barbara, two years my junior, and little Kathleen. Kathleen was only six. We couldn't expect her to do any serious fishing, but nevertheless she, too, wanted to fish, so Timothy Aloysius rigged a pole with a triple-hooked feather gizmo for bait. This thing with feathers was generally fastened behind a spinner and used for casting or trolling. We were fishing close to shore. An offshore wind caused our boat to drift slowly toward deep water. We crossed a drop off, and Kathleen's pole literally doubled. She let out a scream. My dad got a fast hand on that pole or the fish would surely have pulled pole and small fisherperson into the lake. What an exciting struggle ensued! When the monster fish was finally brought into our boat, it turned out to be a seven-pound northern pike, the largest fish that was caught by our group that season. It was almost as long as Kathleen was tall.

My mother baked this beautiful fish and it was delicious. I do believe that the sooner you can eat fish after catching them, the better they taste. I swear that my little sister Kathleen grew an inch on that two-week vacation. She became a champion early in life, and I became a devotee of Minnesota when I was twelve. I loved the lakes and the pungent smell of pine trees.

Now I was back in beautiful Minnesota, doing a play at the Old Log Theater. In the cast of *Not Now, Darling* was a tall, lovely Swede who played the role of a model. Her name was Anita Anderson.

For years I harbored a secret dream that one summer day I would journey to Sweden and find a tall, beautiful blonde on a sun-drenched beach.

Merry Christmas from Minnesota

That dream was never fulfilled, but a variation of it did occur. Instead of going to Sweden, Sweden came to me—in Minnesota. The population of Minnesota contains a large percentage of Swedes. Anita Anderson was one such. Her father came from Sweden; her mother was of Swedish descent. She had been to Sweden twice, and she spoke Swedish. Under the aforementioned circumstances, it was inevitable that I should gravitate toward her as though it were my destiny.

Anita, true to her Viking heritage, had planned a summer in Alaska. Her parents had recently made a trip to the forty-ninth state. Their glowing reports of the last frontier awakened her wanderlust and caused her to book passage to Alaska. Shortly after our first date, Anita left for Alaska, but a flame had been lighted and we kept it glowing with the help of Uncle Sam's mail carriers.

Don asked me if I could stay and do the next play, *Plaza Suite* by Neil Simon. How could I say no?

I spent three months at the Old Log and became convinced that I could make a living in Minneapolis. It's a great theater town, and because there is a talent pool, related work prospered: commercials, industrial films, modeling. As my plane soared up into the sky and headed east, I looked back at Minneapolis and said, "Don't worry. I'll be back." By the time my plane landed at Kennedy Airport, I decided the time had come to check out of New York City. It had been very good to me, but all things end, and I felt it was time to say good-bye. I had a philosophy about living in the Big City. You should either be young and/or making a big buck. If you are neither, retreat to a place where the river of life flows more serenely.

Portrait of an Actor

The TV set in my mind plays endlessly:
Reruns, all reruns: Cheap bars, moondrenched shores
Wives, mistresses, triumphs, failures.
Where is the switch to turn it off?

Give me the maze of an intricate plot,
I'll find the gold of motivation.
The instantaneous moment of reality;
Give me a stage to move on;
Spots, keys, floods to warm me;
My only reality lies in unreality.

36

Au Revoir, Jill Melody

On the return trip, my mind was focused on Jill. I did not waver in my resolve to leave New York, but I didn't know how she would respond to this move.

Jill Melody was waiting for me at the airport with a warm smile, but something was different. It was as though a scrim had dropped down between us. We were looking in different directions. Jill felt that her future was here, in Manhattan. She was young, ambitious, and in step with the tempo of Broadway. I was mature— a has-been, really—looking for greener pastures that were far to the west.

Conversation flowed nicely, for there was much to tell on both sides. In the course of catching up, Jill mentioned that she had met a producer. Whoops!

"Where did you meet him?"

"When I was working the switchboard at Billy's Registry."

"Have you gone out to lunch with him?"

"Yes."

That little jolt gave me the courage to say what was really on my mind.

"Jill, I'm going to check out of New York—permanently."

"Why would you do that?"

"Because I know I can make a living in Minneapolis as an actor, and I like it there. The lakes, the life style, I feel at home there. How would you feel about moving to Minneapolis?"

After a pause she asked, "How's your drinking doing?"

"About like usual."

This served as a reminder, so I went to the kitchen and mixed myself a Scotch and soda. While mixing, I thought, "There's no time like the present. Let's hit her with the big one and find out where we're really at." I took a big swig of Mother Courage and returned.

"Jill, you didn't answer my question. How would you feel about moving to Minneapolis?"

"I don't want to move to Minneapolis. I like it here."

"Okay, let me ask you this. How would you feel about ending our marriage?"

"Why?"

"Because it won't work if we live in different cities, and I am leaving New York. Period."

Jill shed a few tears, but not many—no heartbreak symptoms. I decided to move it.

Next day I called on my friend, Joe Bailey, a theatrical lawyer. When I told him the particulars and what I wanted, Joe said, "Hum! You're sure this isn't just a mood?"

I replied, "I'm positive."

He thought for a minute, then said "Maybe we could get an annulment. How long have you been married?"

"Ever since puberty."

Joe laughed. "I mean to Jill."

"About a year and a half."

"How old are you?"

"Old enough to know better. I'm fifty-six."

"And Jill?"

"Twenty two."

"What if we said Jill wanted to have children but you refused because you have three grown daughters? Would she go along with that?"

"Probably."

"See what she says and get back to me."

"Thanks, Joe."

Joe was able to put through the annulment. It seems to me that marriage is the supreme test for humans in this world. Career is number two in my book. When you put two birds together in one cage, strange things sometimes happen. The twosome may be comprised of two friends or lovers, a married couple, or two roommates brought together by an ad in the paper. There are always adjustments to be made.

Neil Simon made this point with deadly accuracy when he put two poker-playing buddies together in his play *The Odd Couple*, one a slob, the other meticulous. After a couple of weeks, a plate of spaghetti hits the wall. There is one exception to the birdcage theory: parakeets. Their bill and coo inclinations seem to flourish in close quarters.

Although my ultimate goal was Minneapolis, I decided to visit L.A. first. I wanted to see my three daughters, Colleen, Kathleen, and Molly, and my seven grandchildren.

What fun these little people were! They immediately attached themselves to grandpa, and although I said, "I'm much too young to be a grandfather," I loved it. Here was the ongoing, never-ending continuity of life in the form of grandchildren.

Then there was my old friend the ocean, patiently waiting for me, unchanged, breathing, and seething as it flung itself on the sandy shore. The gulls still laughed as they winged their way down the beach. A wonderful feeling of relaxation came over me as I stretched out on the sand, cooled by the ocean breeze, warmed by the brilliant sun.

I called on a talent agent, and he said the magic words an actor loves to hear, "Why don't you hang around awhile, Terry? I think I might be able to do something for you." So I set myself up for a Hollywood siege. First, I needed a flexible job, one that allowed me to walk out at a moment's notice, then return when the theatrical job was completed. Real estate qualified, so I went to work for the Hollywood office of Castagna Realty. Back to the wonderful world of escrows, contingencies, and mortgages. My first transaction was not a sale, but a purchase

A house came on the market described thusly: "2 bedroom stucco with a single car garage. Needs a little T.L.C. $13,500." In real estate lingo, T.L.C. means tender loving care, but what it really means is a hell of a lot of work. The house was located near Melrose and Vermont. It was literally an oblong stucco box that sat on a postage-stamp lot with thirty-five feet of frontage on Raleigh Street. The living room had a fireplace. That and the price impelled me to reach into my checkbook. A mere $13,500 sounds unreal, but this was 1971, and it was a bargain.

My thoughts turned to Anita Anderson. She was now living in San Francisco, where she had a covey of cousins. Our correspondence had been a delight, but now it was time to pursue our romance on an eye to eye basis.

37

San Francisco

Early one Saturday morning I caught a plane to San Francisco. What would it be like to see the lady Viking again? She and that city each have a charm of their own. I had an inner glow of anticipation that wouldn't stop. Was this a romance I had created in my imagination or were we destined to walk down life's pathway together? My reverie was interrupted by the plane's powerful takeoff. Then as we headed north, I counseled myself, "Relax. Let this day unfold as it will. There are two people involved and they must be of one mind."

At the San Francisco airport, I rented a car and drove to Anita's apartment on Castro Street. The door opened and there she stood, tall and beautiful. We kissed and the kiss became quite warm.

Then Anita asked, "Where would you like to go?"

"How about Fisherman's Wharf for openers?"

She said, "Wonderful!"

We bridged our six-month hiatus as though it were a day.

As we drove down a steep hill, we passed one of those quaint little cable cars clanging its way up. At the bottom of that hill we came to Fisherman's Wharf.

We wandered around this unique emporium shopping for a picnic lunch. Our first purchase was a Dungeness Crab, a delicacy from the nearby ocean. The fishmonger skillfully cracked the crab into edibility with his wooden mallet. Then we strolled on until we found a bakery that sold crusty loaves of French sourdough bread. Our final stop was at a grocery store for a bottle of delicious Sauterne wine, a product of the nearby hills.

At this point, time out was called for a coffee break. As we sipped our espressos, I said, "Anita, you know San Francisco better than I, but have you ever been to Muir Woods?"

"No. I've heard of it. Isn't it a redwood forest?"

"Yes. A friend of mine said it was really beautiful. Would you like to explore?"

"Yes, let's."

"After Alaska it might not seem like much."

"No, honest. I'd love to go."

Now we were ready to cross the Golden Gate Bridge. This bridge has been so lauded in song and lore that one expects it to be made of the precious metal. Cross it at sunset and you can conjure up the illusion that it's gold plated. It blends beautifully with the bay's sparkling blue water. Not far from the bridge exit is the quaint little town of Sausalito. On Saturday mornings it sends out a fleet of small boats with white sails to capture the winds that frequent the bay. We were tempted to linger here in Sausalito, but Muir Woods was our destination and the promise of a gourmet picnic spurred us on.

Muir Woods National Monument bears the name of its founder, John Muir, a naturalist who had the foresight to save these beautiful redwood groves for future generations. Redwood forests are nature's cathedrals. Even their silence seems larger than life. Here and there a shaft of light penetrated the pervasive shows like a spotlight. These super trees dwarf us and are capable of stirring up a bit of humility in our souls. However, the awesome effect of this giant forest wasn't so overwhelming that we lost our appetites. In fact, our appetites assumed gigantic proportions, befitting the trees we sat under.

What a beautiful day this was. No striving to make small talk, it flowed by like a lazy river. When the sun set, we felt very close. I told Anita about my funny little house on Raleigh Street and invited her to come see it.

"Next weekend?"

When I boarded the plane for L.A. I was able to answer that big question.

"Yes, I think we are destined to walk down life's pathway together."

38

Joshua Tree

At this time my daily consumption of Scotch was, well, more than it should have been. I remember one evening we attended a little party at Bill Lally's home. About midnight we got up to go home.

Bill said, "You don't have to leave yet, do you, Terry?"

I paused for a moment, then said, "Not really."

So we talked and sipped till 3:00 A.M. The next day I had an appointment with a photographer to have some new theatrical pictures taken. The night's activity showed in my face; the pictures had to be tossed out.

Shortly after this photographic fiasco, Anita and I had a disagreement. Nothing big, really, but because I was half loaded, I overreacted. I fulfilled the need for some histrionics in my life by making a scene. Next day I apologized, but Anita said she had never been around anyone who drank as much as I did and she didn't want to spend the rest of her life in this fashion, so she returned to Minneapolis.

Now I was alone. Not really. I had my bottle of Scotch. It had become my companion. I thought about the winos in New York City. Derelicts, with ruined lives, staggering aimlessly around, sleeping in puddles of their own urine. Disgusting! Was that where I was headed? I felt that if I could just get away from telephones and the frustrations of life I could kick this habit, for I now was highly motivated. So I decided to go camping in the desert.

Drive east from L.A. to Palm Springs, then turn north, and almost immediately you will begin a gradual ascent that continues for the next forty miles. Almost imperceptibly, you climb to the high desert. At four thousand feet elevation, Joshua trees begin to appear—strange-looking mutated plants that would appear to be the result of a cross-pollination between a cactus and a pine tree.

To me, Joshua Tree National Monument looks like an area where hundreds of years ago an atomic bomb exploded, blowing away the top soil, exposing high rock formations that thrust upward, tossing boulders around willy-nilly, leaving a surface of sand and gravel. Here in this forbidding terrain the Joshua Tree flourishes. Not clustered like a forest, but spaced carefully to avoid overcrowding. The kind of topography one might expect to find on a distant planet.

The days are sun-drenched and hot, but the nights are temperate and star studded. The sky is spectacular. Due to the pristine atmosphere, every star in the entire universe sparkles like a jewel.

It was here, in Joshua Tree that I pitched my tent and set up camp—"Far from the madding crowd's ignoble strife." No phones, no phonies. A few lizards, a distant bird song, a predawn serenade by coyotes, and enormous stretches of uninterrupted silence, long walks, and uninterrupted sleep.

I spent a week in nature's rest home. I stopped drinking. The cure lasted for twelve years. I stopped smoking. The cure was permanent.

During my desert retreat, I wrote a poem which I entitled "Solitary Imbiber":

Between twin boulders, dawn had poured
A delicious glass of rosé wine.
In the cool, sanctified desert air,
I drank the vintage offered me,
Then gourmandized stillness, sun and wind;
'Til sunset opened its hidden store
Of golden sherry and pink champagne:
Wanton inebriate! I! Alone!

I returned to my stucco hacienda. It felt lonely, but the ghost of Anita lived there, and somehow that helped. I called my friend Walter Brooke. He had previously told me about a theatrical group he belonged to called Theater East. Now I was desperately looking for things to do, so I joined Theater East—a group of professional actors who met each Monday night to perform scenes, critique same, and thereby hone their acting skills.

If you saw *The Graduate*, a motion picture that starred Dustin Hoffman, you will perhaps remember Walter Brooke. During the party scene, it was he who took Dustin Hoffman aside and said, "I have only one word to say to you—plastics!" It's not easy to become famous with a one-line part, but Walter managed it.

During the time I was active at Theater East, Walter, his fiancée Yvonne White, and I performed Strindberg's *The Dance of Death*. It's a haunting play that lingers in my memory. I can still see Walter doing the sword dance with his military boots and drawn sword.

I busied myself with real estate, and business picked up. I kept in touch with Anita by phone and letter. One day I wrote:

Dear Anita:
Three weeks have gone by since I stopped drinking and smoking. I feel secure in my new way of life, because each day I am rewarded by the way I feel and perform. Perform, in this case, means to sell real estate, but that's not a new world for me. As a radio announcer I sold everything from Wheaties, breakfast of champions, to O'Sullivan's rubber heels for shoes. I shall never forget the punch line for that commercial: "Remember O'Sullivan, America's number one heel." I guess it runs in the family. Not really, I hope. Actually I'm a good sole.

I know that alcoholism is in my genes, but failure is not, so I will succeed in this.

Now about you, Anita. I'm grateful that you had the strength and courage to leave me. I knew, vaguely, that my drinking was getting out of hand, but as Scarlet O'Hara said, "I'll think about that tomorrow." It took a real earth shaker, like your leaving, to make me realize what was happening to me. I love you, Anita, and I really miss you. You have done much more for me than you realize. I don't know if your objective was to change me, but I have changed because of you. All my love.

The weeks slowly turned into months. Then I received a phone call from Sue Wehman, a theatrical agent in Minneapolis.

"Terry, guess what. 3-M wants you to do an on-camera spokesman in an industrial film."

"You mean come back to Minneapolis?"

"Yes. Is it possible?"

"Sue, let me put it this way. Even if were impossible, I'd do it."

The next two weeks went by slowly but smilingly.

When I got off the plane in Minneapolis, Anita Anderson was standing in the back row of the group of welcomers at the airport. Well, why not? She could see over most of them and she was not pushy by nature. I gave her a long, passionate kiss. Perhaps a bit too long and too passionate for a Scandinavian, in front of all those people, but that's the way I felt, and I'm not Scandinavian. Then we walked off, arm in arm, as though there had been no space between.

We had dinner at Lord Fletchers, a delightful restaurant on the shore of Lake Minnetonka. It was here that we had dined on our first date. Next day I met her parents: John Anderson, a good-looking, slender Swede from Sweden with Swedish accent, yet, and Char, a warm, smiling, plump schoolteacher. Char was her stepmother; her real mother died when Anita was twelve.

Later, I asked Anita what her folks thought about me.

She said, "Oh, they liked you. My dad said, 'Isn't he kind of old for you?'"

I replied, "Your dad is right. You're the same age as my oldest daughter, Colleen. But that's one of those immutables engraved in stone."

The film went swimmingly. Industrial films are used as selling aids or for teaching. They are the nuts and bolts of picture making.

So now it was time to return to L.A. Anita drove me to the airport. We were both rather quiet. Our good-bye kiss was warm and full of longing. It was difficult to let go and walk away. Before I disappeared into the plane entry, I turned and we waved good-bye. I took her image with me on the plane. On the return trip, Anita occupied my mind completely. I thought back over our hours together. I had forgotten how bright she is and how lovely she looked sitting across the table in a properly lighted restaurant. I had begged her to come back to California, but she couldn't seem to say yes, nor did she say no. We were back in limbo land.

However, I had one card left to play in this game of hearts—marriage. True, she would be wife number six, but remember the old platitude? "If at first you don't succeed, try, try again." I'm sure the person who first uttered those words of wisdom did not have marriage in mind. But since said person did not qualify his pronouncement, we assume that it would work with marriage as well as with any other of life's many pursuits. Hopefully each failure would teach the participant not to try that caper again, much like the hot stove method of acquiring knowledge.

By the time our friendly captain informed us we would be landing in twenty minutes, my mind was made up. I would propose to Ms. Anderson by telephone. That at least would be a first.

39

The Bells Are Ringing

*A*nita said "yes" to my proposal. We arranged to meet in Las Vegas where we would be married. Anita drove her Volkswagen all the way from Minneapolis. I flew in from L.A. We met on a Friday evening. I was fresh as a daisy after my hop, skip, and a jump plane trip. The bride-to-be was road weary, dusty, and cranky.

I smilingly asked the inevitable question, "How was your trip?"

She unsmilingly replied, "The state of Nebraska smells like cow manure."

This reply shook me a bit. I thought, "Maybe I should have listened to my dear mother." After the collapse and failure of my fifth marriage, Amy begged me, "Please, Terry, don't get married again." I assured her that I wouldn't dream of doing such a stupid thing. Now, here I was, in the gambling capitol of the world, eager to roll the dice again.

A shower and a Manhattan, made with Southern Comfort, restored Anita somewhat, but she was not bubbling and nervous as you would expect a bride-to-be to be. This would be Anita's second marriage. This would be my sixth attempt at connubial bliss, and I wasn't bubbling either, but I was a tad nervous.

My daughter Kathleen got married in Las Vegas in a chapel, and it was a lovely wedding. The marriage didn't last, but as yet, most ministers do not issue fifty-thousand-mile warranties with a marriage certificate.

I wasn't prepared for the bleakness of the civil ceremony that awaited us that fateful Saturday morning. We were nervously sitting in straight-backed chairs in a bare office setting. A door burst open and a noisy bridal party spilled out. Right on the heels of the last person to exit, the civil

servant person thrust his head out the door and shouted, "Next!" like in a
dentist's office.

I said, "I guess that's us."

We stood up, tried to smile and walked hesitantly into the marriage
factory.

The civil servant asked if we had any witnesses. We apologized for
our lack of preparation.

He said, "That's okay," and shouted, "Betty! Mabel!" Two smiling
secretaries appeared, as if by magic—our professional witnesses.

The civil servant positioned himself behind his desk on which stood
an artificial flower in a dime-store vase to create an aura of romance. He
glanced up from his text to see if everyone was properly placed, then he
started to read. Midway through the service, Anita started to cry. Without
missing a beat or fumbling a word, our trusty civil servant opened a desk
drawer with his right hand and extricated a box of tissues. He offered it to
the tearful bride, who quietly accepted one as though this moment had
been rehearsed. I couldn't help wondering, "Do these tears flow from the
emotion of this momentous moment, or do they flow from regret, or even,
possibly, fear of the future?" This speculation caused me to be late for one
of my cues—embarrassing for an actor. Then he pronounced us, and the
congratulatory response of our paid witnesses was refreshing.

As we left his office, me smiling, Anita blowing her nose, we heard
"Next!" reverberate through the building. I saw a young couple arise and
I so much wanted to shout, "Go back! Go back!" But I bit my lip and
trudged on.

As we stepped out into the bright sunlight of a Las Vegas day, I found
myself humming a Peggy Lee song, "If That's All There Is"; but that wasn't
all there was. Our Volkswagen had a sparkling white parking ticket on its
windshield. Las Vegas is a swinging town. They're not concerned about
gambling or he-ing and she-ing, but they're very upright and moral about
their parking violations.

As we drove back to our hotel minus rattling tin cans and honking
horns, I said to Mrs. O'Sullivan, "Well, Anita, we've got nowhere to go
but up. Let's go for it." So we did—and have. The by far worst wedding
has turned out to be the by far longest marriage. Twenty-three years with
a twenty-two-year-old bonus, our daughter, Elizabeth, a graduate magna
cum laude from Macalester College. Sometimes people win when they
roll the dice in Las Vegas.

Next day we drove back to L.A. and took up residence in my funky little house on Raleigh Street. I returned to Castagna with renewed

determination to list, to sell, and not to talk about the client that got away. Anita picked up a secretarial job and we became the couple that lives down the street. "You know the ones I mean, the older man with the tall, attractive wife."

Anita turned out to be good with a paintbrush, and the restoration of Raleigh Street proceeded apace.

One sunny California day I was planting some petunias in the front yard of my Raleigh Street estate. An old timer, out for his constitutional, stopped to watch me.

Leaning on his cane, he asked, "Did you buy this place or are you renting it?"

"I bought it—with my G.I. loan."

"G.I. loan. I was in the First World War, but they didn't give us anything like that. Which war were you in, the Korean?"

"No, I was in the Second World War."

(A pause)

"Who were we fighting?"

"Hitler. Hitler and the Japs."

"Oh, yeah, now I remember. What's your name?"

"Terry O'Sullivan. What's yours?"

"Bump. Everybody calls me Bump."

"Nice to meet you, Bump."

"Yeah."

Then he activated his cane and walked off.

I thought, "Why didn't you ask him where he got the name, Bump? Oh, well, next time." But there wasn't a next time. I never saw him again. A reminder to do it now. There may not be a next time.

40
Minnesota, Here We Come

*I*n the Hollywood office of Castagna Real Estate, our two top sales people were in trouble with the IRS. The problem is you don't get a regular salary, but then when you make a sale and receive a big check, no deductions are taken out. All of a sudden, it's April 15, and the balance in your checking account is surprisingly low. Yes, you bought a new car, but that was absolutely essential because you wanted your clients to think you were successful.

Real estate slowly but surely takes over your life. It demands all of your time and most of your energy. It does have one thing in common with acting: they both have big disappointments—auditions you lose when you thought you were perfect for the part, house sales that collapse just before the closing.

There are definitely more laughs to be had in theater, although black comedy does, on occasion, occur while one is peddling real estate. One sunny Saturday afternoon, I loaded my station wagon to o'erflowing with a Chinese family that included five children. I carefully took them through a lovely home that seemed to answer their many needs. They liked the house, and as we drove away, our conversation became animated with barter discussion. I drove about two blocks, then stopped at a stop sign, at which point Mrs. Toy let out a blood-curdling scream that reverberated through the Hollywood hills.

"What's the matter?" I implored.

Mother was already gushing tears as she sobbed, "We left little Ling back at that house!"

I made a precarious U-turn and back we roared to retrieve the abandoned, tear-stained child. Ah, yes, all in a day's work. No, they didn't buy the house.

One frustrating day at the office, after a big sale collapsed, I impulsively picked up the phone and dialed my friend, Don Stolz, at the Old Log Theater.

I said, "Hi, Don. You don't happen to need an actor, do you?"

Don said, "I can't offer you steady employment, Terry, but I could use you in the next play."

"What is the next play?"

"It's a farce, *No Sex Please, We're British*."

"That sounds like a ball. When should I be there?"

"First of July."

"I'll be there. Thanks, Don. Really, thanks."

Anita was overjoyed. Minneapolis is her home.

Fathers Day 1973 was celebrated at Raleigh Street. The house was filled to overflowing with my children and grandchildren. My daughter Kathleen Bienz, her husband David, and their three cuties: Bobby, Brian, and Daveena. My daughter Colleen Dawson and her handsome pair, Dan and Shannon. My daughter Molly Stuman and her two charmers, Doug and Romy. I looked around and thought, "What have I done? Behold this multitude." Anita and I had collaborated on a turkey dinner, which turned out great. I got my camera and started shooting. It was a wonderful gathering. When it was over, I sat down, somewhat stunned. I'm afraid I had been like Daddy Warbucks, not around very much—now I was leaving again.

Next day I started to unload my camera, but something seemed wrong. I took it to the camera shop. The man went into the darkroom to unload it. When he returned, he said, "There's nothing wrong with the camera. The problem is in your head. You forgot to load it."

I will spare you the dreariness of packing, then driving across the desert, and magic-carpet you to the Old Log Theater, where comedy reigns supreme.

British farce tends to have stock characters. There is usually a pompous ass, an executive-type fellow who attempts to restore order to a rapidly deteriorating situation. Nature has endowed me with the necessary qualifications to play the pompous ass.

There is usually a mother's boy who has memorable lines like, "I should be getting home. Mother will be furious." This part was played in deadly earnest by Ross Bickel. Ross had a timorous, hang-dog quality when I read him the riot act. Sometimes it was difficult for me to maintain my stern visage when I looked at those downcast eyes. One Saturday night when the audience was especially boisterous, I had to walk away from him. When I tried to speak, I would start to laugh. In theater lingo this is called a break-up. The audience loved it.

At this time, Ross was married to a gorgeous brunette, Loni Anderson. Loni was much in demand as a model in Minneapolis. She was a lovely creature who smiled easily and often. I was surprised when I learned she had a daughter named Deidra from an earlier marriage. She seemed too young to be a mother. Loni did a show at the Old Log Theater, *The Patrick Pearce Motel*, and she did light up that stage with her presence.

Also in the cast of *No Sex Please* was Jerry Newhouse. Jerry, when playing farce, seemed to be slightly confused by the strange events that were whirling around him. He was a very funny actor.

No Sex Please, We're British turned out to be a laugh riot. Oh, God, it was fun to be trying for laughs instead of begging for real estate listings.

During the run of this madhouse farce, Jerry Newhouse invited the cast over to his apartment for a Sunday brunch. Along with the scrambled eggs and sausages, Jerry served bloody marys, an insidious concoction that tastes like a drink one might purchase at the health food bar, but watch out—hidden in the tomato juice is a time bomb.

Some time during the afternoon of the aforementioned Sabbath, Ross's time bomb exploded. He and Loni had a little disagreement. Ross, in a fit of towering rage, threw a punch—not at Loni's beautiful face (God forbid he should do that). No, he gave the wall of their apartment a punch. Unfortunately, his fist contacted a stud. You know, one of those upright two-by-fours that hold the wall up. That evening he came to the theater with his arm in a sling. His hard right to the upright broke his hand. This unfortunate accident caused us to lose a couple of really good laughs.

At one point in the chaotic proceedings, I am giving Ross a stern lecture; he is backing away from me. Meantime, Cindy Subby is crawling around the stage on all fours looking for her lost earring. As Ross retreats, he contacts the crawling Cindy and falls backwards. Ross could do a bit of tumbling, so he did a spectacular backward fall. This bit didn't work with a broken fist. We lost that laugh.

Later in the play, he rode Margaret Christopher across the stage piggyback. She would gallop through the upstage door leaving Ross hanging on the door frame. It was not easy to hang there with two hands, impossible with one, so we said "bye-bye" to that side splitter as well.

The lovers got over their quarrel, Ross's hand healed, and the handsome twosome headed for Hollywood, the land where many are called but few are chosen.

I will never forget the first time I saw Loni on television with blonde tresses. It was shocking because she had been such a definite brunette when I knew her; but what the hell, it worked.

The camera loved Loni; the stage loved Ross. That made it tough to maintain togetherness. Ross came back to the Old Log Theater. Loni stayed on in Hollywood to fulfill the ultimate dream—stardom. That's show biz.

No Sex Please, We're British was followed by *The Happiest Million-aire*. I played Anthony J. Drexel Biddle, the millionaire. This was my favorite role on the stage of the Old Log Theater. To be a millionaire for even 2½ hours out of the twenty-four was richly rewarding. Then to put on gloves and box a round on the stage, plus singing a few lines from an opera. What more could a ham want?

Ann Blager played my wife. She is remembered at the Old Log as a good actress and as the creator of a classical spoonerism. During the run of *The Mousetrap*, she made an imperious entrance, then with projection and precise pronunciation, she made a blatant presumption. She said, "This is Monkswell Manor, I see-pume." This blending of suppose and presume into a new word, "see-pume," shocked and delighted both cast and audience. Yes, it was a spoonerism, but it was also the creation of a new word which is still used in Minnesota.

One day I had lunch with Don Stolz at the Old Log Theater. Chef Denny Henderson, who was new at the Old Log, asked my wife, "Who was that man I saw having lunch with Don—the one who was dressed so nicely?"

Anita smiled and replied, "That's the man who married me."

"Oh," said Denny, with awe and respect, "I didn't know he was a minister."

Ever since then, Denny has called me "The Rev," and I in turn call him "The Chef."

On the 6th of December, 1973, Elizabeth Amy O'Sullivan was born. My fourth daughter. I was hoping to have a son, but I figured the dear Lord knew I liked girls, so he surrounded me with daughters. Having a child late in life was a wonderful experience because I had more time to devote to her. When I was younger, I was so focused on my career that I didn't give my daughters as much attention as I should have. Then came the divorce, which widened the gap. This time I made a a promise to myself that I would not walk out of this marriage. This time I would stay, and I have.

One day Joan, Don's wife, invited me to lunch. I knew that something special was happening because Joan was not in the habit of inviting me to lunch.

Cast of The Happiest Millionaire
Front row: Terry O'Sullivan and Ann Blager
Back row: John Stolz, Christine Anderson, and Peter Stolz

So I asked, "What's up, Joan?"

She said, "It's a surprise."

When Tuesday came, Joan picked me up at my home. I remembered that Rotary met on Tuesdays at the Old Log Theater, so I figured it might have something to do with that. We drove past the Old Log. I didn't ask what this was all about, because I wanted to show that I'm a man with savoir faire.

We chatted about other things and wound up in the parking lot of the Guthrie Theater. Now I was really curious. Here we boarded a shuttle bus and were transported over to the Woman's Club. It was abuzz with gray-haired ladies. Joan took me to a room next to the main dining room. There were about twenty women seated at tables.

"Do you see anybody you know?" asked Joan.

I scanned the faces and said, "No."

She smiled and asked, "Mary Stuart?"

Now I looked intently and said, "Oh, my God!" It had been eighteen years since we worked together. Joan was right. This was a surprise, spelled with capital letters.

During lunch, Mary and I traded stories about our days on "Search for Tomorrow" when we were Arthur and Joanne—much to the delight of the ladies. After lunch, Mary gave a talk about her life as an actress and her thirty some years on "Search for Tomorrow."

Driving back to Excelsior, Joan Stolz said, "You know, Terry, that's what you should do. Write a speech about your life in the theater."

The more I thought about it, the more convinced I became that Joan was right. So I wrote a speech and delivered it one Monday night at the Old Log Theater. Everyone had a wonderful time, so flush with that triumph, I found the courage to sit down and write this memoir. Thanks, Joan.

41

To Catch a Thief

T HE INTRUSIVE RINGING of the telephone interrupted my reverie, and
I said to myself, "Now who could that be?" The answer to my question erased the frown from my face and replaced it with a smile.

The voice on the other end of the instrument said, "Hi, Terry, this is
Tom Gilshannon."

"Hi, Tom, what's up?"

The answer to this question caused my smile to grow even broader.

"I recommended you for a job."

"Thank you, Tom. Does it pay?"

"It should pay rather well. You'd be part of an investigative reporting
team, working in a nursing home."

"You've got to be kidding."

"I know it sounds bizarre, but some of the residents of this nursing
home have been robbed lately. A diamond ring, clothes, money. They suspect that one of the employees is responsible. So Channel Five has decided
to do an exposé on robbery that occurs in nursing homes. They're looking
for an elderly man who would be willing to go live in a nursing home as a
bona fide resident. Once inside the establishment, he would be able to set
a trap and hopefully catch the thief. The nursing home management would
not be informed. The entire operation would be strictly undercover. What
do you think?"

"What about yourself, Tom? Aren't you interested?"

"I would be, but they think I'm too young."

"It's that smile, Tom. You smile too much to play an old man."

"How about you, Terry? Are you interested?"

"Yeah, it sounds exciting as hell to me, I mean to work as an undercover agent. I've never done anything like that, but I'd sure like to try. Who do I contact?"

"Get in touch with Joel Grover, Channel Five."

"Thanks, Tom. Thanks for thinking of me."

I hung up the phone and headed for the nearest mirror. I looked intently. The face that stared back at me was that of a man who had seen seventy-eight summers and God knows how many winters and hard falls. If I lost this audition, it wouldn't be because I looked too young.

"Don't darken under the eyes, Terry. Just go as you are."

I was interviewed by Joel Grover and Jay Kolls of the KSTP investigative reporting team. They were impressed with my acting credits, and my age was great, seventy-eight. Next question, could I prove I had sufficient income that would enable me to live in a nursing home? My social security check plus a couple of union pension checks got me over that hurdle.

Jay said, "Terry, you look pretty healthy. Do you take any medication?"

"No, but my memory is starting to play tricks on me."

"Good, use that when you get to the nursing home."

"Looks like you're our man," said Joel. "Now let's do a little brainstorming. We need to come up with a scenario for you. Let's start with the reason you decided to check into a nursing home. Any thoughts?"

"I could say that my wife died about six months ago and I'm finding it very difficult to live alone. The truth is, Anita did come close to dying several years ago when she had an aneurism of the brain. This affliction has a high mortality rate. She's one of the lucky ones; she made a full recovery."

"Good. The closer you stay to the truth, the better off you are."

"Next, we need someone to come visit you every day or so. We were thinking that maybe Jay here could be your grandson. What do you think?"

"I don't see why not. My oldest grandson is about Jay's age, even looks a little like him."

"Good. We need to get a cane for you. Jay, would you take care of that? A word of caution: don't get too involved with anyone in the home, employee or patient. The more you talk, the more apt you are to say the wrong thing."

I decided in my own mind that I wouldn't think of myself as living a lie. Instead I would think of this assignment as an ongoing improvisation. In acting class we did lots of improvisations. Our instructor would give us a very brief plot, tell us our emotion and our action, and what we were trying to achieve. Then we would get up on the stage and do a scene. It taught us to think on our feet, and sometimes these improvisations were surprisingly good. Improvisation is a rather formidable sounding word. Actually, we did improvisations when we were children, but in those days we called them Let's Pretend or Let's Play Like. "I'll be the daddy and you're the mommy." Remember?

The nursing home required a physical examination before I moved in. We made an appointment with a clinic on Lake Street that said they could squeeze me in the next day.

The physical examination was rather lengthy. The last step was an interview with Dr. Jensen. She had a warm, friendly manner and I immediately felt at ease in her presence. I eagerly recited my medical history: measles, mumps, melanoma, appendectomy, and prostatectomy. Then she asked me why I was going into a nursing home.

I paused, looked at the floor, then responded, "My wife died about six months ago and I find it very difficult to live alone."

"May I ask the cause of your wife's death?"

I took a deep breath, then said, "She had an aneurism of the brain."

"Oh, that was very sudden, wasn't it?"

Her deep concern and sympathy involved me in the scene. My eyes began to water and my throat tightened, at which point I said to myself, "Stop it, you ham, enough already." She could see I was fighting back the tears. She patted me on the shoulder and said, "I'm sorry." This ended my improvisation with Dr. Jensen. P.S.—I passed my physical. Now I was ready to check into Casa Del Sol nursing home. I was interviewed by Ms. Blevens, who questioned whether I was a candidate for a nursing home. She felt I might be happier in a limited care facility, and suggested a few.

I countered with, "Well, you see, my grandson located Casa Del Sol and made all the arrangements. I feel that I should at least give it a try. My commitment is just for a month, and during that time I would have a chance to look at some of the other facilities you mentioned."

Ms. Blevens seemed happy with that explanation, so now I was a full-fledged patient at Casa Del Sol with my own room, down at the end of the hall.

That afternoon, my newly adopted grandson, Jay, arrived with some of my favorite items to make me feel at home during my stay: a couple of pictures to hang on the wall and my favorite bedside lamp. The lamp had a video camera built into it. The night stand on which the lamp rested contained a videotape machine. The door of the night stand was locked to discourage the curious from peeking. A small wooden box was strategically placed on a table. It contained my watch and a couple of ten-dollar bills.

When someone stepped between the lamp and the box, the camera was automatically activated. Our trap was now set.

I will not soon forget my first night at Casa Del Sol. I had trouble getting to sleep. Then about 2:00 A.M., someone started to wail. It was a frightening sound, lonesome like a wolf's howl. It didn't last long. I imagine the nurse on duty administered a sedative to the unhappy patient, but I had one hell of a time getting back to sleep.

Each day my grandson would drop by to visit me, and while I stood watch at the door he would check the film to see if there had been any sticky-fingered visitors during those times when I was out of my room, watching TV, or wandering aimlessly about, cane in hand.

Dining was not something I looked forward to. The food was passable, but it reminded me of eating at the automat in New York City, where people sat at tables but seldom spoke to each other. My favorite dining companion was a little old lady who wore a knitted cloche hat. She had a warm smile, but she was stone deaf, so I didn't have to attempt a conversation. We just smiled at each other and ate quietly. Once I heard a nurse feeding a reticent patient. The dialogue went like this:

"Open your mouth," she said. "Chew it. Now swallow it."

The lines were delivered like a drill sergeant taking his troops through their paces.

The highlight of my nursing home stay was when one of the nurses would bathe me. I sat in a chair; then a machine lowered me and the chair into a tub of nice hot water. Then the nurse washed my back. It was heavenly. One could easily get hooked on being bathed each evening.

I looked forward to my adopted grandson's daily visits, for they were my link to reality. Four days and four nights had slowly come and gone with no attempted robberies, so it was decided that I would visit my grandson for the weekend, thus providing a potential thief with a better opportunity to loot my treasures.

It was during my weekend hiatus that the hidden camera did its duty. We returned to Casa Del Sol on Monday morning .

My grandson smiled when he reloaded the camera and said, "I can hardly wait to see what we've got here."

Next day Joel and Jay came to my room, and Jay said, "We've got it, Gramps. Not one but two thieves. A double header."

I was interviewed by Joel Grover in front of the nursing home, and this interview became a part of the TV program. Then I packed my bag and checked out. I took one last look at Casa Del Sol and silently said a little prayer: "Dear God, please keep me from ever spending time a nursing home." I know they're a necessity in our modern world, but they leave a lot to be desired.

The exposé was entitled "Betrayal of Trust." It was presented on the ten o'clock news and turned out to be a top-flight investigative reporting program. It was our hope that it would alert people to the risk of leaving valuables with their loved ones when they go to live in nursing homes, and we hoped that nursing homes would be more diligent in checking the backgrounds of their employees.

42

Curtain

O N THE SEVENTH DAY of the seventh month, in the year 1995, I celebrated my eightieth birthday. It was quite a celebration—a double
header, in fact—a party on the Fourth of July and a party on the seventh. To be mobile and alert after eighty summers, and God knows how
many winters and hard falls, is cause for celebration. So we did it. Big time.

At some point during the birthday celebration, my friend, Bob Reid
asked, "What's your secret, Terry?"

"Secret?"

"I mean, you're doing great for eighty. How did you manage it?"

"Maybe it's my genes; but I do believe in three things: you are what
you eat, exercise or your joints will rust, think positive thoughts."

"Okay, but could you elaborate on that just a little?"

"Did you ever garden?"

"Yeah, I love to garden."

"Then you know that poor soil produces poor crops. If you add to this
soil the essentials it lacks, your next crop will show dramatic improve-
ment. In this respect, we're no different from a plant. Maybe that's why we
call a dried-up person an old prune, or a cute girl a tomato."

Watch a basketball game. Talk about fantastic action. Our bodies are
created for action. Without it, they rust. When I become slothful, and I do,
I remember Grandmother O'Sullivan. Her health was failing when she
was forty-five.

The doctor said, "Mrs. O'Sullivan, I want you to get out and walk
every day." So for the next fifty years, Grandma Julia walked to and from
Mass every morning and sometimes twice on Sunday. She died when she

was ninety-four, and I expected to see her walk to the cemetery—striding too. She moved it.

The mind does affect the body. You know what happens when you really get mad. You can feel the adrenaline flow. Norman Vincent Peale's book, *The Power of Positive Thinking*, has helped me in my quest for a positive outlook. You remember that song, "You've got to accentuate the positive, eliminate the negative, latch on to the affirmative, don't mess with Mr. In-between"? That says it with brevity.

"I'm not a tower of strength. I become careless and lazy, but always I come back to my trio of beliefs and start again."

For ever so many years, I have wanted to write a book. Now I have done it. I know my family will appreciate it. I would love to have read a memoir written by Cornelius O'Sullivan, my grandfather who came from Ireland—the one who ran a saloon down at Ninth and Walnut—or a book by Robert Nesch, my grandfather who came from Switzerland. Those had to be exciting times. Right after the Civil War. Imagine coming to a new country and building a life for yourself. Grandfather Nesch did very well. He started a paving brick company in Pittsburg, Kansas, and became modestly wealthy; had ten children, then divorced his wife and married his secretary. Guess it runs in the family. Both grandfathers petrified their livers with daily drinking and died long before I was born. Both grandmothers made it to ninety-plus.

The question is, "How does one end a memoir?" Life goes on. Slower, I'll admit—much slower—but it does go on. I was searching through some papers, various things I had written in the past, poems, essays, desperately looking for an ending, when I happened on to a letter from my daughter, Elizabeth. She wrote this just after she graduated from high school. Thanks, Betsy; you're the writer in this family.

My Father

On dewy June days of the past, I didn't analyze much.

You were my dad. And people said, "It must be kind of unusual having an actor for a father—a man with so much life in his past and present." I always regarded them as somewhat stupid. Though I let the situation pass with as much grace as I could muster. You were just my dad—the only one I'd ever known. And who was anybody to say you were unusual?

But summer's sun is the downfall of transient dew. And a year or so ago, it passed into anger.

But, Dad, I loved you then too. One night, last summer, I remember well. Mom was gone, and you made that excellent chicken I like so much. You cut strawberries for dessert. Spent all that time, carefully cutting those little red strawberries and letting the juicy sections drop into a bowl.

I thought about that even as I answered your attempts at conversation with noncommittal and hurtful indifference.

I don't think you remember that. I almost hope not.

But I remember. I remember you and your strawberries.

My anger passed on, too. What you did was wonderful. So wonderful that I can't reach to touch the currents of its breeze—even standing on my toes! But for some reason, awkwardness lingers after anger goes.

Life passes on, and I've had to start thinking, what shall I do with mine? I don't think I want to spend my life tame and confined behind a desk. Sterile and stagnant. I don't know…

But I think I want to act.

At least…it flickers in my mind as a possibility.

So with changed perspective, I've been watching you, Dad. You entered a field of dreams and met success. That is one of the greatest triumphs ever told in any of the many, aged volumes of life.

You became another kind of victor by going to A.A. And in the beauty you see and create, you are the conqueror of all the troubles ever laid in your path.

I know this because it shows in every flower you tend, every strawberry you slice.

Dad, I love you. Sometimes our relationship is a little distant. But it's true, always. And no matter what happens, I want you to remember that.

Happy Birthday, Dad!

Love, Betsy

Elizabeth is now the editor of *St. Louis Park Revue*, a local newspaper.

The Poet's Corner

Garden of Eden?

Garden of Eden?

If all our days began at twilight,
Our rendezvous a candle lit cafe;
There to sit and contemplate your assets;
A rapt audience to your slender fingers
Twirling round a long-stemmed glass.
To dance endlessly, all rhythms, tempos;
One with the saxophone and drum:
To dine gourmandizing delicious dishes;
Bewitched by your lustful appetite.
To make love, love encompassing
All activities: all dreams and fantasies,
The epitome of conquests;
The why of wherefore.
If this were all—all of life;
No carping neighbors, no vicissitudes or stress;
Just one lazy, smiling serpent:
"Oh, why did he eat that tainted apple?"
"Eve dared him to, I guess."

Student of Volcanos

Good Morning! Woman, with green eyes and smoldering fires!
Nature heard, with delight, that you would pass this way;
So she bedecked, bejeweled, and colored, lavishly.
Her incorrigible son, the breeze, is rather fresh, I think;
Does he not touch you here and there, in sensuous manner?
Grant me, your Lover, the enviable freedom of the wind.
See, how the generous sun explores the hillside?
I, too, am a generous son, who can warm and explore.
Beyond the green hills stands the purple mountain wall;
See where the peaks rise, rounded like your breasts?
Do restless, old volcanos smolder 'neath those peaks?
Fortuitous, isn't it, that during my scholastic days
I discovered how to waken restless old volcanos?
Good morning! Springtime!
Was there ever such a day?

Moon and Sea

Love, that you and I might be moon and sea,
That I might rise up from you, golden,
And light your every wave;
Journey through my appointed space,
And descend into your waiting arms.

No matter what space between,
You would feel the pull of me,
And somehow I would sense your give.
Thought I left you for a night,
A glimmer of hope would shine in your tomorrow,
And that would be me, striving,
To grow, to attain perfection,
A full moon floating above a shimmering sea.

Forgetful

Enchantress, you left your pearls
On my dressing table,
Crumpled and lifeless, pretty but dull;
How they glowed last night
When they encircled your exquisite neck;
Come to think of it, so did I.

Voluptuary

Woman your body is a ripe bud,
Ready to burst with the next sunbeam;
What terrific pressure it exerts
On tiny hooks and delicate stitches;
Each thread is taut and straining,
Striving to keep you in the confines
   of its civilized domain:
Pagan, you should have lived in the
   age of fig leaves:
Thanks, for choosing this moment—
   And me

Our Playground

Look, love, night is waving to us,
See him in the darkly swaying trees?
Follow him? Our playground is open!

Let us build beautiful sex rockets,
That burst in the face of the moon,
And softly sprinkle the astonished stars;
Then let us twine and intertwine,
Float, thus, down the dark stream:
Weave with soft gossamer threads
Dreams strange, ephemeral fabric:
Construct a towering levee against light,
That we may float, thus, forever.
Wake! Dawn has penetrated our levee.
Place your finger in the light leak:
Help! Help me! Hold back the dawn.

Summer Storm

When at long and lovely last,
The storm of love had raged and past;
Quite sultry seemed the summer air,
Like damp and tangled grass, your hair'
A lake had formed between twin hills,
And spilled down curves in tiny rills.

Your navel was extremely wet,
A tiny rain barrel filled with sweat.

Persistent Salesman

How can you sleep so blissfully?
Someone is knocking at your door!
Wake up, Love, and let him in!

I swear he won't go away.
He's a persistent salesman;
But his wares are most unique:
He's a purveyor of instant joy,
Mad intoxication—with no hangovers.

The knocking persists! Please, Love,
Let him in! He won't stay long;
Then we can both go back to sleep.

Loser

I've lost my pretty Teddy Bear,
My long and sexy Teddy Bear,
My snuggle bunny Teddy Bear:
How can I sleep?

Remember?

The sting of sweat in the eyes,
The taste of blood from a cut lip;
The heart pounding, gasping struggle
Up a steep mountainside of orange poppies,
Then the thundering herd of buffalo
That crushed our poppies with black satyr hooves
And swept us over the steep cliff
To crash in the surf below:
Whose lip was bleeding? Yours?

Clouds of Confusion

Clouds of confusion are blowing through my sky,
Troops of clouds, majestically sailing,
Like great armies silently moving
To reinforce some far-off storm
Immobilized, I watch and yearn.
I struggle to weigh the anchor of you,
I open my unfilled sails and wait.
When will my craft sail again,
And toward what unknown destiny?

Autumn

The painted hills admire themselves
In the still mirror of our lake,
Sunset peeks warmly over their shoulders;
Frost is lurking in the shadows;
Our world is in escrow, winter waits for possession.

You turn to me with a summer smile,
But a cool breeze touches my cheek;
Now I feel the quiet ache of autumn,
That hides in the heart of the hills.
I smile at you, but where are the words
That flourished in our summer?
You are looking far beyond the hills.
Do your green eyes see another springtime?
Mine see only winter.

Insomnia

The alcoholic flame has sputtered out,
I ache for rest,
In my loneliness I embrace sleep:
Then from the dark corners of my mind
Dart weird creatures of the subconscious,
Dwarfs with fiery eyes and hairy hands,
Who pervert life into hideous travesties;
They torture, warp, distort.
I see your frightened face,
I hear you scream my name,
My eyes open, but you are not there;
So I wander through the desert of insomnia
And find you everywhere.

Restless

Autumn stalks the hills like a painted Indian;
The sun, a worried parent, gives one last glance
At its restless child and quietly closes the door.
From out the shadows come dark winds and ghostly frost.

Let me build bright fires on the hills of October,
And dance with the leaping flames,
Flinging strange shadows on the startled trees;
Let me wail at the moon with luminous eyes;
Let me fly through the silent sky of cold stars,
A bewildered wild fowl, lost from its comrades;
Let me race down the gloomy avenues of fear,
And falling, feel the icy hand of frost;
Let me hurl stones from the high cliff
And hear the hungry waters gulp them down.

The night of me mutinies against my day;
My body yearns for the warm fire of whiskey;
I hear the click of high heels down a dark street,
My hands ache to hold a beautiful woman.
Desire sails my vessel, I follow the neon lights.

Jealousy

My mind accounts for your absence;
But my emotions won't listen;
Doubts beat frantically upon the doors,
They crash through my mental defenses,
And engulf me in jealousy and bitterness.

Masochist

Thirsty, I'm so thirsty,
I ache for that exquisite taste —
Delicious drops of salt water
That swim from my eyes
To my eager lips.

Sadist

Whips? How gauche and unrefined.
Not when one has words like mine.

A well turned phrase—the tears do well,
The proper question—there's a Hell.

Place them on the verbal rack,
Find a nerve and watch them crack.
Whips? No! No! They're too barbaric.
Try my way; it's esoteric.

Lonely

Night has come again, so softly;
Without warning, without sound;
Day softly whispered around me;
Now the whispering has gone.

Untrue?

Last night I was untrue, to you,
All through the dark hours,
I danced and slept with pain,
Glittering pain, with needles, twists and flame.
Locked in each other's arms,
We danced sadistic symphonies,
No lovers ever close as we,
Not even thought could wedge between.
The aching candles flickered out at dawn,
And morning found me quietly alone.
I heard day hurry up and down the street,
Racing its engines, honking its horns.
Now shadows in the corners reach out for night,
And in darkness I reach out for you.

Wild Oats

Amber sea of wild oats shimmering;
Rippling waters, awash in the air:
Cornucopia, aching for filling;
Springtime's promise, too pregnant to bear:
Summer's maturity—growth now suspended;
Seeds in their gold husks, trembling there.
"How do I harvest my bountiful sowings?"
"You don't, dear farmer, they harvest you!
Fair?"

Dancing in Space

I'm orbiting beautifully in space,
The stars are my tiddlywinks;
That isn't a man in the moon,
It's a beautiful woman.

I sneer at you earthbound peasants,
With your shovels, mops and smog;
While I dance at the end of my rope.
Just one question. How do I re-enter?

Evening

Sunset's orange lantern
    hangs above the sea,
A sea gull's graceful
    silhouette epitomizes me.
Against the wind,
    in fading light,
Forever seeking thee.

Memorial Day Night
1971

The smoked glass mirror of our lake
Transforms distant lights into shimmering jewels.
We stand in darkness on the shore
Listening to waves as they whisper to silent stones,
Watching skyrockets climb the ebon sky
To explode, dazzlingly, in space.
They descend like clusters of falling stars.

"Do skyrockets remind you of orgasms, love?"
"Yes." A bewitching smile. "But they're not as good!"

To order additional copies of this book,
please send full amount plus $4.00 for
postage and handling for the first book and
50¢ for each additional book.

Send orders to:

GALDE PRESS, INC.
PO Box 460
Lakeville, Minnesota 55044-0460

Credit card orders call 1–800–777–3454
Phone (612) 891-5991 • Fax (612) 891-6091
Visit our website at http://www.galdepress.com

Write for our free catalog.